EVERYWOMAN'S BOOK OF NUTRITION

JANE HOPE
DR. ELIZABETH BRIGHT-SEE

McGraw-Hill Ryerson Limited

Toronto Montreal New York St. Louis
San Francisco Auckland Bogatá Guatemala
Hamburg Johannesburg Lisbon London Madrid
Mexico New Delhi Panama Paris San Juan
São Paulo Singapore Sydney Tokyo

To Ian and See . . . liberated enough to
appreciate liberated women.

EVERYWOMAN'S BOOK OF NUTRITION

Cover photo of Jane Hope courtesy Gerald Campbell Studios.

ISBN: 0-07-548460-9
1 2 3 4 5 6 7 8 9 10 THB 1 0 9 8 7 6 5 4 3 2

Printed and bound in Canada

Canadian Cataloguing in Publication Data

Hope, Jane.
  Everywoman's book of nutrition

Includes index.
ISBN 0-07-548560-9

1. Women—Nutrition.   2. Women—Health and hygiene.
I. Bright-See, Elizabeth, date II. Title.

TX361.W55H66   641.1'02'4042   C82-094084-4

TABLE OF CONTENTS

A FEW WORDS OF EXPLANATION

We decided that a book written mainly for women was the place to give the feminine pronoun equal time. Thus, you will find that we use she as the general pronoun. Any combinations (i.e., s/he) are still awkward in prose, and our bias is to compensate for other decisions made in favor of the opposite gender.

The metric system is coming slowly. This is making us think about our food and about nutrition in a different way. But not too differently—it's not us, our food, or how we cook that is changing, but simply how we measure things. For example, a kilogram of chicken (or of our weight) is slightly over two pounds. A pound is really 0.454 kilograms (kg) or 454 grams (g). One ounce of weight is about thirty grams. But one fluid ounce is about twenty-five milliliters (mL). That's one of the advantages of metric—fluid and weight ounces will no longer be confused. Because we are still in transition, we have given most measures in both units; cups and milliliters, ounces and grams, and so on.

Probably one of the last conversions in the nutrition area will be food energy—calories to kilojoules (kJ). One calorie is about 4.2 kJ. That means that protein and carbohydrates have about 17 kJ/g; fat, 37 kJ/g; and alcohol, 29 kJ/g. Kilojoule is now being used in scientific and government publications and is being taught in the schools. But its acceptance is otherwise not yet widespread, so we have chosen to use "calorie" until "kilojoule" becomes a little more familiar. We refer to low-energy diets, however, rather than low-calorie or low-kilojoule diets, because that's what calories and kilojoules are—simply measures of energy we receive from our foods.

1 THE SPECIAL WOMAN

On hearing the title of this book, the first reaction of many men has been to accuse us of blatant chauvinism. Why focus on nutrition for women? they ask. Surely your nutritional needs are no different than ours.

Certainly, proper nutrition is important for both sexes. But our needs, whether they be emotional, physical, or nutritional, do vary from our male counterparts. Our other needs or desires have been explored in depth by sociologists, psychiatrists, therapists, and the media. But less attention has been paid to our nutritional needs. The extent to which dietary requirements of women differ from that of men has only recently been recognized. Until now, we only really received dietary attention when we were pregnant or were breast-feeding. The importance of a well-balanced diet for that particular time (which may add up to a very small part of our lives, if indeed it applies to us at all) has been understood since early studies connected nutrition with health.

It's now confirmed, however, that women should increase certain nutrients during other physiologically demanding times in their lives. In general, our nutritional requirements are different and are more variable during our life cycle than they are for men. Our bodies demand extra nutrients because of menstrual losses, the Pill, pregnancy and lactation, and probably menopause. For example, from the time we are teenagers until menopause, we are more susceptible than men to various nutritional anemias. Pregnancy, of course, is another significant physiological development with potentially serious nutritional effects. In addition, there are important patterns emerging in our population as a whole, many of which have a great impact on women's life habits.

Studies reveal an increasing casualness in living, a greater degree of self-expression and self-centeredness. There are more older people, mostly older women, in our population. Working women have emerged as a strong social force. Marriages are taking place later in life; many women are becoming first-time mothers at a later stage in life than in previous generations. (Interestingly, until recently there was a decline in the birth rate, but this is slowing.) Families are much smaller, more single people are living alone, and the popularity of what might be called "companionate marriages" is on the increase—there is even a newly coined word, "co-vivant," used to describe live-in companions.

And there is no denying the rising affluence in North America of the middle class. We're spending less on food at home than Europeans, and we're swinging more and more into the fast-food lane.

These trends cannot help but affect our general nutritional well-being. Our life styles dictate how we live and how we eat. As a result, perhaps because of the strong awareness of the connection between diet and disease, nutrition has become an important word in our vocabulary, a subject of controversy that influences the welfare of the country, industry, governments and, of course, the individual consumer.

Yet, nutritionally, we're in a state of flux, caught in the cross-currents of conflicting information. Perhaps the single most significant trend of women in the total nutrition picture, according to a survey done by *Women's Day* magazine, is the tug between the changing values of today and the rigidity of traditional nutrition concepts. The "new values," as they are termed—with their emphasis on self and self-fulfillment, together with women's new role, our relaxed and casual life styles, far less formality and rigidity than even just a few years ago—are at odds with our traditional role as the homemaker. Our earlier mandate was "three squares a day," balanced meals at set hours with a careful menu in which certain foods were appropriate for certain meals. A cold chicken leg for breakfast? Never.

We're now adopting new and different concepts of nutrition. And the concept of nutrition for women is definitely among these. Throughout this book, we examine the current trends, attitudes, and contradictions that influence how we eat. We look at women's different needs during different parts of their life cycle. We know from responses to our weekly column that you also want information on diet and weight control. You want to know how to eat well on less money, how to plan balanced meals, how to handle the snacking syndrome. In this book, we discuss these and many other topics. But one of the most significant factors underlying these questions is women's changing role.

We now play a greater part in the social, economic, and political parts of our society. But some of the old responsibilities have stayed with us. Often we're trying to be too many things to too many people; in other words, playing too many roles. "Role-overload" is a real problem and will continue to be until we recognize that trying to be "wonder woman" is self-defeating.

The first step towards being healthy, physically, mentally, and emotionally, is to learn self-evaluation and how to set priorities. What is really important to you? (One woman's revelation came when she realized that being a good mother didn't mean that she had to cook all her children's meals.) Being successful doesn't mean you have to be a gourmet cook or have to entertain lavishly. If you want to, fine. If not, remember that good nutrition can be supplied in the most simple meal. Often, the company— friends getting together—is just as important as what is served.

Society is changing...and so are eating patterns. Descriptive terms abound; for example, we now have "The Grazing Society." This catch phrase doesn't imply that we nuzzle up to a field of straw. What it describes is the more active life style of today's families—each family member involved with various activities, each of a different nature— that prevent them from dining together. Mom perhaps has an early evening course, while Dad may be attending a service club meeting and the children are involved in hockey practices or ballet lessons.

The emerging superclass, a new term given to the two-career family, will strongly influence the eighties, setting marketing trends and shaping consumer tastes for years to come, according to Money Management Institute. This new, high-income group is comprised of families where the husband and wife work on the professional, managerial level. This separates them from other two-paycheck couples.

About one of every four families belongs to the superclass today, with incomes over $29,000 (in 1980 dollars). By 1990, forty percent of families will belong to this class. What caused this growth and what effect will it have on health? The Baby Boom children have grown up and have reached their peak earning power. More women are in the labor force and are *staying* there, creating dual income families. They've postponed marriage and family to further their careers, and, as a result, they reach managerial levels and contribute a higher and higher percentage of the family income.

Estimates show that *sixty* percent of the take-home pay in the United States will be controlled by the two-income family in 1990. This new group of affluent adults, many of them female, will have a dramatic effect on the economy and on standards of living.

These new life styles and higher incomes demand foods designed to meet the family's varied schedule. Hence, the food marketplace has grown more complex over the past few years. In the twenties we had fewer than 1,000 items from which to choose. Today, we face more than 10,000 items each time we visit a supermarket. But perhaps because nutrition is a relatively new, fast-changing science, the knowledge and understanding of food and nutrition has not grown at the same rate. We face a vast array of fresh, frozen, canned, pouch-packed or dehydrated foods, and we have to decide how to get the best nutrition from our food dollar. Not an easy task, but by reading certain chapters in this book, you'll be able to interpret the maze of labels and plan meals quickly and economically.

Women are generally more health-conscious than men. That is, we are often more concerned about food and other factors that affect our own health and that of those important to us. Health is important to success in anything. As well as indulging ourselves in a new record or reading a good novel, we must "indulge" ourselves in good health. This is part of the philosophy of "enlightened self-indulgence"; we must take care of ourselves before we can properly care for or contribute to anyone else. Women's liberation has led to a "Me Too," not a "Me First," attitude.

All too often, diet recommendations for North Americans tend to be geared to healthy nineteen-year-olds. Obviously, these recommendations are not appropriate for a sixty-five-year-old. That's why we've looked at each stage of women's lives so critically and attempted to explain specific nutritional requirements for those specific stages. We examine the dietary hazards or potential nutrition pitfalls and suggest an eating strategy (ways to avoid or overcome any potential problems). Some chapters may be more applicable to you than others. Reading the book from front to back is not what we had in mind. Select the information that applies to your particular phase and role in life.

In the second chapter, adolescence is examined. Prior to adolescence, boys and girls grow and develop in much the same way and require essentially the same amount of nutrients. During adolescence, however, there are definite changes in body composition, and separate recommended nutrient intakes have been set for eleven- to fourteen-year-old males and females.

But growth rates vary widely during this period, so it is hard to predict when one individual will have specific nutrient requirements. We do know that the diets of most teenage girls are poor—and are growing worse. Dieting to the point of endangering health is a growing problem of teenage girls. And many have become fanatic calorie counters; they are more concerned with calories than with nutrients when planning what to eat each day. Many teens eat several meals a week at a fast-food outlet, and as a result diets tend to be high in fat and calories and low in essential nutrients like iron and vitamin A, which the teen girl needs. This becomes a real problem when a teen becomes pregnant. (One study, incidentally, estimates that in the United States, each night over 2,000 teenage girls become pregnant.)

From adolescence right through to menopause, women are more likely to develop anemia than men. Approximately forty percent of women aged twenty-five to fifty have inadequate iron intakes. The iron needs of menstruating women is about fourteen milligrams per day, but it's difficult for the average North American adult or teen to get that amount from a normal diet.

The average North American diet gives you about six milligrams per 1,000 calories—and the average intake for women is about 1,550 calories a day. Therefore, you're getting only about half of what you need. As well, iron absorption from these food sources varies widely. Only about thirty-five percent of iron from meat, fish, and poultry is absorbed. On average, only about ten percent of the iron you consume is absorbed. Long-term folic acid (iron) deficiency results in megaloblastic anemia—which causes problems with cell duplication, and, therefore, growth. We deal with this problem in the eating strategy on p. 18.

In the past few decades, a new nutritional hazard for women has surfaced: oral contraceptives. The extent of their effect is dependent on the type of oral contraceptive, your age, the length of time you've been on the Pill and how healthy you were at the time you began to take it. Any borderline nutritional problems will be heightened by the Pill; specifically, vitamin B_6 and folic acid, and to a lesser extent vitamins C and B_{12}, riboflavin, and thiamin requirements will change. We discuss how to handle any possible problems in Chapter 8.

We also discuss pregnancy and lactation. The old adage that the fetus will obtain all the nutrients needed from the mother, no matter what she eats, is simply not true. And so, weight gain, calorie intake, alcohol and other drugs, and the increased need for certain nutrients are thoroughly examined. We also talk about what happens when you decide to nurse. The nutritional cost to you includes calories required to synthesize lactose (the sugar in milk), proteins and fats, as well as the nutrients taken from your blood in milk production. Again, a balanced diet is the key: our eating strategies will help you meet the increased calcium demands and the need for essential vitamins, iron and other minerals.

Women who work away from home—and those who work at home—have to face changing life styles, especially in eating patterns, both for themselves and for their families. We discuss the problems of the executive menu, coping with food budgets, what to eat and serve for breakfasts, and so on, in Chapters 5 and 6. Meals around the family dining room table, while not obsolete, are a far less common phenomenon than a decade ago. We eat more than one out of every three meals away from home now. That number will increase shortly to one out of every two. The main meal away from home is lunch. The kids may brown-bag it, and probably so do you, from time to time. A couple of times a week, supper may come from a local Chinese or Italian takeout, or a fish 'n' chip spot. Or you may take everyone out to supper. The fast-food industry is growing at a rate of fifteen percent per year—hamburgers, chicken, pizza, and hot dogs of all types are staples. (Watch for tacos and potatoes of every variation from skins to stuffed to join the ranks of fast foods.) We flock to these outlets in droves because they're fast, clean, fairly cheap, filling, and they cater to youngsters. Millions of kids are growing up to love the flavor of a Big Mac with special sauce. A spinach soufflé just doesn't have the same appeal. Fast food isn't going to disappear, so we've included, in Chapter 2, some advice on making the most out of those meals.

There is more to food than simply eating. Meals serve an important function in today's nuclear family—as a time when you can come together with the kids. And a business lunch can clinch a deal. We turn to food as an entertainer, and even as an indication of social standing. Discussions of what trendy new restaurant is in, what cooking class you're attending, what new piece of cooking equipment you've bought, where you shop for your fresh sorrel, are frequently as important a topic as interest rates.

In 1980, we spent $12 billion in Canada alone to feed ourselves. Yet there's a dichotomy. We also spend millions jogging, joining fitness centers and weight reduction clinics. Therefore weight management is discussed in almost every chapter. As you'll see, we don't believe in miracle diets; instead, we tell you how to cut down sensibly—the rest is up to you.

Surveys show that the woman who works away from

home spends as much as fifty percent more on her family's food than she would if she were at home. She shops hurriedly, failing to take time to make out a menu, and often running out of basics, which she must replenish from a nearby convenience store. She often buys instant mixes, sends out for food, or takes the family out for supper because she's too tired to cook. For this group, we discuss how to cut back on unnecessary spending and suggest a few quick recipes. We stress that organization is the key. And so is a willingness to spend a half hour or so in the kitchen at night or a couple of hours on the weekend preparing and freezing weekly meals. We suggest planning around a set of reliable, fast, main course recipes, with simple desserts like fruit and cheese. We also discuss the importance of involving *everybody* in meal preparation. Shared responsibility lightens your pressures in the kitchen.

Members of the older generation are one of our most important national resources. While we've recognized that a child is not just a miniature adult but an individual undergoing constant development, we're just now realizing that an older person is not simply a young person who has lived longer. We stress that blanket statements cannot be made about nutrient requirements; they simply can't cover all age groups. As we age, our body changes; so do the functions of the organs and, therefore, our nutrient needs. For example, osteoporosis—the weakening of bones—is a common problem among the elderly. Aging also imposes certain changes in the gastrointestinal tract. And many elderly also have weight management problems. In Chapter 9, we look at the special problems of the older woman.

We've emphasized special nutritional requirements

for different stages of your life. But we give you some general advice, often, throughout the book.

FACTS AND FALLACIES

Mention nutrition today, and almost anyone will be willing to give you advice based on their current pet theory. But this advice may not fit what you heard from someone else the day before. Even qualified nutritionists sometimes seem to give conflicting advice. This often happens because there are several different types of recommendations around—designed for different purposes.

The oldest of all types of nutrition recommendations are the Canadian Recommended Daily Nutrient Intakes (RDNIs) and Recommended Daily Allowances (RDAs) in the United States. Sometimes they are not understood very well, and they are often misused (particularly by those who want us to believe that we should be taking vitamin and mineral supplements).

The RDNIs and RDAs are merely statements of amounts of protein and certain vitamins and minerals that will meet the needs of almost every healthy person in the country. They are not the same as *requirements*. Therefore, studies reporting that North Americans are not receiving the recommended intake of nutrients do not prove that these people actually have deficiencies.

We all need protein, minerals, and vitamins (and energy, but we'll discuss that later) to stay healthy. But the amounts *you* need will be somewhat different than those needed by someone else, even someone the same age, sex, and size. However, as no one knows exactly how much each individual needs, the closer your intake is to the recommended amounts the better chance you have of meeting your needs. If you happen to eat less than the recommended amount of vitamin A or vitamin C for a day, or even a week, you're not likely to develop a deficiency. But if you continue to eat this way for a long time, the likelihood that you will develop a deficiency increases greatly. For most of us, our requirements for protein, vitamins, and minerals are not nearly as high as the recommended amount. (Only in very rare cases will a healthy person need more than the recommended amount.) The adage, "If a little's good, more is better!" just isn't true for nutrients.

In fact, the latest version of the U.S. RDAs emphasizes that there is an optimum intake of nutrients. They have set the recommended intakes, which are very close to Canadian RDNIs. The RDAs also give upper limits for many nutrients, amounts that may lead to toxicity. Such toxicities are most likely to occur with fat-soluble vitamins (A and D especially) and trace or micro-minerals such as iron, zinc, and copper.

The recommended intake of energy (or calories) is somewhat different. This is set at the average for the whole population. About half of us will need less, and the other half will need more. Here, your own weight is the best indicator of the correct amount.

But few of us start off the day by planning to eat fifty grams of protein, 800 mg of calcium, and so on. Tables of recommended intakes are not very practical in our day-to-day eating.

That is why the recommended nutrient values have been translated into foods. This translation is called *Canada's Food Guide*, or the *Basic Four* in the U.S., simply logical groupings of foods according to the nutrients they contain. Breads and cereals supply protein, fiber, minerals, and B vitamins. Fruits and vegetables are sources of vitamins C and A. They also contain fiber, some minerals, and B vitamins.

Milk and milk products, of course, are our main supply of calcium. They also give us protein, riboflavin, vitamin A and, in fortified products, vitamin D. The so-called meat group also contains eggs, fish, beans and peas, and other sources of good quality protein, minerals, and vitamins.

The other recommendations we are most familiar with are from the American Heart Foundation. They state that to reduce the chance of heart disease we should decrease our intake of fat, particularly saturated or hard fat. They further recommend that we cut our cholesterol intake by about half to 300 mg a day.

An expert committee in Canada some years ago generally agreed with the American Heart Foundation. It did not, however, emphasize the strict reduction in cholesterol intake. The reason for this is that most of us get the majority of our cholesterol from eggs, and eggs are marvelous food, supplying high-quality protein, easily absorbed iron, vitamin A, and B vitamins. We wouldn't like to see them eliminated from the diet—particularly diets of older people—unless a very strict therapeutic diet was prescribed by a physician because of high blood cholesterol.

Being aware of the importance of health and of nutrition to health is not enough. You must have facts. And sometimes these are not easy to get. The guidelines we've discussed are an excellent aid, and this book is another. But you may need additional help; perhaps, for instance, if you're following a special therapeutic diet. In that case, find out about the nutrition resources in your own community.

It may not be easy at first to identify a qualified nutritionist. There are no regulations controlling the use of this title. And some people seem to think because they enjoy eating food, or perhaps have read a little bit about food in general, that they automatically become nutrition experts. (Does riding in a plane make you a trained pilot?)

If you are talking to a "nutritionist," ask about her background. What's the level and type of education? What are the professional associations to which she belongs? Beware of anyone who claims to have the only answer or states that she is being unfairly condemned by other nutritionists or health professionals.

The title "dietitian" is the only one that is protected. Only those who have met certain education and training standards of national and provincial organizations may use this title. Any registered and qualified dietitian can give you correct nutrition information. Some provinces (Ontario and British Columbia) have a free Dial-a-Dietitian service. The number is listed in your phone book.

Another reliable source of information is your local public health nutritionist. Some provinces, Ontario and Alberta, for instance, have a group within their provincial dietetic associations called "Dietitians in Private Practice," which offers nutrition counseling for a fee. Or you may ask your doctor to refer you to a hospital out-patient dietitian. (A portion of this fee may be covered under a provincial health scheme.) For additional information, check the Yellow Pages under associations for your local dietetic association, or call your local hospital's dietary department or the health unit in your area.

2 THE GROWING WOMAN

Teenagers in Western societies are subjected to a great deal of physical, social, and psychological stress. While we can't begin to deal with all of these areas, we do want to talk about some of the physical changes, about how these relate to nutrition, and about how nutrition affects your ability to cope with the other demands of this trying (and exciting) time of life.

We can't say whether boys have an equally difficult time. But we do know that adolescence is the time when the female changes more rapidly and perhaps more dramatically than the male. You may grow several inches (centimeters) and gain ten pounds (five kilograms) in a short time, fill out rapidly, and worry about getting fat. Menstruation, no matter how coolly explained in health education classes, is still rather a shock and takes a while to get used to. And as an added insult, you may have skin problems—acne and pimples.

All of these changes mean that the nutrient needs of females begin in adolescence to be different than the needs of males (and will never again be exactly the same). As well, male and female eating habits are quite different. Recent studies confirm what has been generally believed for many years; that diets of children become progressively worse as they enter the teens. Lousy is the only word to describe the diets of many teenage girls. Boys seem to fare better, not because they are any more intelligent about nutrition, but just because they eat a lot more food— and by luck rather than good management score higher on the nutrition scale.

Why should teenage girls be one of the least well-fed groups in North America? Part of the answer is that your need for all nutrients has increased rather dramatically from the preteen years. These nutrients are needed because adolescence is the second fastest growth period in your life (only the growth of infancy is faster). In many instances, you need more nutrients than a grown woman.

The other part of the answer lies in what determines your eating habits. This is likely to be body image, peer pressure, and availability of food—practically anything but a sound knowledge of nutrition. Even girls who are aware of good nutrition rules may not find it easy to follow them.

Growing up means becoming aware of your own needs and taking the responsibility for seeing that they are met. This chapter will help you do that.

THE PHYSICAL CHANGES

Not only are you growing rapidly, you are also maturing physically. That means that your body composition and function (as well as size) are changing.

Menstruation is the most obvious and dramatic illustration of maturation. It has an immediate impact on the requirement for iron. Males and nonmenstruating females lose less than one milligram of iron from their bodies every day. The blood loss during each menstruation leads to additional iron loss—and the recommended intake of iron jumps from eleven to fourteen milligrams a day (we absorb only about ten percent of the iron in our food, therefore our intake should be ten times our actual requirement).

The iron that's lost each month must be replaced or iron stores (found mostly in our livers) will be robbed. If that happens, not enough hemoglobin will be formed, not enough red blood cells will be produced—and you will end up with anemia. Anemia is a worldwide nutrition problem; women of child-bearing age in North America aren't immune. Indeed, anemia is listed as one of the major nutrition problems of women—from adolescence to menopause.

Anemia can be caused by many things—excess blood loss, deficiency of vitamin B_{12}, folic acid, or iron. Most of the time, it's possible to determine the cause of the anemia by the size, shape, and color of red blood cells as well as by other clinical tests. Lack of iron is the major cause of the anemia problem in North America.

Anemia exists because our food supply does not really contain a great deal of this essential nutrient. There are a few foods with reasonable amounts of iron, such as beef liver and heart, enriched cereals, oysters, prune juice, dried beans, and other red meat products. Many other foods (green peas, chicken, eggs, tomato juice, tuna) contain small quantities of iron. Milk, milk products, and highly refined foods (sugar, oils, and shortenings) have very little. Despite what you may have learned at your mother's knee or from Popeye comics, spinach is not a good source of iron. Spinach does have a great deal of iron but this iron is bound to oxalic acid so we can't absorb much of it. The same is true for other vegetables such as Swiss chard, beet tops, and rhubarb.

Eating according to either the *Basic Four* or *Canada's Food Guide* does not necessarily mean you'll get enough iron. Some researchers have even suggested that there is simply not enough iron in the food supply to meet all our needs.

Eating Strategy   *Iron*

To make certain you're getting all the iron you need, eat a good serving of one of the high-iron foods at least once a week and two to three servings of the moderate sources every day (see page 48). Remember that iron from animal products is generally absorbed better than iron from plant products. If this is impossible, or if your doctor finds that you have anemia (iron-deficiency type), we recommend that you use a supplement. Get a good supplement—ferrous sulfate, gluconate, or fumerate. About ten milligrams a day is enough to supplement the iron already in your food. Don't waste money on "organic" or "natural" iron. The only organic iron of any use would be the kind found in meats, and it's much too expensive to put in supplements. Ferrous sulfate or ferrous fumerate is absorbed and used just as well. (One advocate of "organic" iron told us that the advantage of his product was that you could take all you wanted without worrying about an overdose. That only means that very little of this iron was absorbed in the first place.)

SMART NUTRITION

It's a bit of a paradox. About one-third of teenage girls are overweight, but they, along with their slimmer friends, may not be getting all the nutrients they need. An abundant supply of calories does not automatically mean a good supply of nutrients.

Studies show that teenage girls may not be getting the calcium, vitamin A, riboflavin, and thiamin that they need. This situation may be due to:

- the increased nutrient needs during the teen years
- low total food intakes
- monotonous diets
- skipped meals and lots of snacks

Sometime between the ages of twelve and eighteen, your weight will nearly double. When this happens and how much time it takes varies from person to person. But most of your growth will occur in two to three years, usually before you're sixteen. During this time you'll need a lot of nutrients and energy, in some instances more than when you're grown (except during pregnancy and lactation). All nutrients are important, of course, but calcium, vitamin A, riboflavin, and iron—the very nutrients that are often low in teenage girls' diets—are major requirements.

If you're restricting your food intake either to lose weight or to try to keep from gaining, your chances of getting the nutrients you need are pretty small. In your early teens, your intake should never be less than 1,000 calories; in the late teens, it should be at least 1,400 calories. If for some reason you have been given a medically supervised lower calorie diet, you will need a good multivitamin-mineral supplement.

What is the cause of so much nutritional trouble? Erratic eating habits. While some teenage girls have the standard three meals a day and eat no snacks, most tend to skip breakfast and/or lunch and tend to snack a lot. In the United States, one-fifth of all teenage girls don't eat breakfast. An equal number don't eat lunch.

Skipped meals cause two problems: you're not giving your body the supplies it needs to function efficiently, and you may become so hungry that you overeat later in the day—say after school. Even a breakfast of coffee and donuts doesn't last until lunch. People who start the day this way have low blood sugar levels by midmorning. They take a long time to make decisions, can't exercise for long periods, and may have tremors after they exercise.

Also, teens who eat good breakfasts tend to consume less total food over the day. It is now believed that protein foods such as milk or cheese consumed at breakfast can alter brain chemicals so that we feel less hungry over longer periods.

Have at least 300 calories at breakfast. This should include a whole grain or enriched cereal or bread, a protein source such as milk, eggs, cheese, peanut butter, and probably a juice or fruit for vitamin C. The vitamin C helps the absorption of the iron in the bread or egg. Breakfasts *don't* have to be conventional: eggnog, milkshakes, bran muffins with cheese, even a cold chicken leg or piece of pizza with a glass of milk and an orange are healthy alternatives.

The same principles apply to lunch. French fries and a soft drink won't serve you very well. A sandwich or another piece of chicken or pizza with an apple and milk will help keep you awake through those afternoon classes.

SNACKING AND FAST FOODS

And what about snacks? They seem to be here to stay. It's estimated that teenage girls get twenty percent or more of their total calories from snacks. But before we can say whether that's good or bad, we have to distinguish between snack foods and foods eaten as snacks. Snack foods are generally high-calorie, low-nutrient foods promoted solely as snacks. They are seldom used at meals. If they were the only foods used as snacks, we might be concerned. Studies have found that while soft drinks, salty snack foods, and candy are among the snacks eaten by teenage girls, so are bakery products, milk and milk desserts, fruit, bread, and meat. Unfortunately, girls snack on milk less often than boys, but they do eat more fruit.

The point is not snacking itself, but what is eaten as snacks. Our bodies generally don't care when they get the nutrients—at a meal, or from a snack. There is evidence that snacking, or at least several small meals a day, constitutes a good way of eating. The opposite extreme, gorging (one or two very large meals each day), leads to the release of a large amount of insulin. In rats, and perhaps in humans too, the calories in those meals are very efficiently deposited as fat—a condition we'd all prefer to avoid.

The snacks teenage girls eat are not as nutritious as foods eaten at meals. Generally, snacks contain more carbohydrates, about the same amount of calcium and magnesium, but less of all the other nutrients. The amounts of iron, niacin, and vitamin B_{12} in the between-meal foods are especially low.

Is it important that between-meal foods be completely nutritious? It depends. It depends on the total energy (calories) and the total nutrient intake of the day. For example, studies have shown that there isn't much protein in snacks, but our total daily protein intake generally exceeds our basic needs. These studies found the same to be true for vitamin C, vitamin B_{12}, niacin, riboflavin, thiamin, and vitamin A. On the other hand, snacks contain nearly as much calcium and magnesium as regular meals do, but our total intake equals only two-thirds to three-quarters of the recommended amounts. The total intake of calcium and magnesium contained in foods is low. Our iron intake is low for the whole day; the iron derived from snack foods is especially low.

Snacks should be considered as part of the whole day's intake. You should emphasize foods high in calcium (milk and milk products) and in iron, both in your snacks and regular meals. But only turn to high-calorie–low-nutrient foods—snack foods—if they are not replacing other more nutritious foods (and if they won't mean too many calories for the day).

We can't discuss snacking without some mention of fast foods or quick service foods. These have become a major component of North American eating—and have become far more than just snacks. While most fast food meals are generally not nutritional disasters, they are usually high in calories, salt, and sugar. For example, a large hamburger, a milkshake, and french fries contain about 1,000 calories. They contain a lot of protein, have an adequate amount of B vitamins, but are especially low in vitamin A and vitamin C (and in calcium, unless milk, a milkshake, or a cheeseburger are included).

Indulging in fast foods every day is not the way to good eating habits or nutritional health. But that doesn't mean you have to avoid them entirely. Try a variety of fast foods rather than just one or two, and select different items each time. As well, try the new items that are now being added to fast food menus—salad bars, soups, frozen yoghurt, even raisin snack packs. Often, breakfast items such as juices are available all day.

Eating Strategy   *Teens*

Follow this pattern as your daily eating guide.

FOOD	SERVINGS/DAY	NUTRIENTS
Milk products	3-4	protein, calcium riboflavin, vitamins A and D
Whole grain and enriched breads and cereals	3-5	protein, fiber, B vitamins and minerals
Vegetables	2-3	vitamin C, vitamin A and fiber
Fruits	2-3	
Meats or other high-protein foods	2	protein, B vitamins and minerals

It's amazing how simple this eating strategy is. And it adds up to only about 1,200-1,400 calories, unless you really work at having only such high-calorie foods as french fries, high-fat meats, and high-fat milk and cheese. If you're a typical teen, the food you probably should include more of is milk. Milk products contain the nutrients which are most likely to be low in your diet. With the availability (and popularity) of all types of delicious yoghurts, perhaps this is beginning to change.

You can be very creative with fast foods. Cheeseburgers fit three categories; meat, bread, milk (and vegetable if they have tomatoes and lettuce). Peanut butter, tacos, pizza, and nut breads also contain some essential nutrients.

ACNE

Common acne (*acne vulgaris*) is a burden to many teenagers (although it is not completely limited to this age group). It may appear as only a few pimples that disappear spontaneously or lead to broad infections and sometimes to scarring. Diet has been commonly blamed for acne. But all studies indicate that food plays little or no role in this condition. You should avoid any foods, though, that seem to cause your acne to flare.

Hormonal changes that occur in adolescence cause glands (called sebaceous glands) on the face, and sometimes on the arms and shoulders, to become active. They secrete a substance called sebum. The sebum dries out and blocks the glands. Bacteria begin to grow, and pus develops. The bacteria also break down fats to produce fatty acids. When the pocket of pus is broken, the fatty acids spread in the surrounding skin, causing inflammation and scarring.

Usual treatment involves avoiding greasy cosmetics and washing the face daily with soaps, sometimes special soaps containing either antibiotics or agents that dry the skin. A sun lamp or direct sunlight may also be used to dry the skin, but light should be used carefully, to avoid sun-

burn. Plugs of sebum (called comedomes) should be removed by a doctor or family member every two weeks. In
more severe cases, hormones (estrogen and progesterone)
are sometimes given to suppress the activity of the sebaceous glands; antibiotics are used to decrease the bacteria.

Three nutrients have been used in the treatment of
acne: vitamin A, zinc, and polyunsaturated fatty acids.
Retinoic acid (a type of vitamin A) is sometimes applied to
the skin as a cream or gel. This causes the skin to dry in
three to four weeks. Retinoic acid has also been used as a
supplement. One study showed that the excretion of sebum
decreased dramatically with its use. Even the water-soluble
retinoic acid—vitamin A—however, can be toxic, so if
you're using retinoic acid you may develop such side effects as dry eyes and mouth, and headaches.

If you use retinoic acid on your skin, avoid direct sunlight, as you'll sunburn easily. In some animal studies,
retinoic acid applied topically increased the production of
skin cancers. Whether this also occurs in humans is not
known. But retinoic acid should be used only in severe
cases and should *never* be used without medical supervision.

The use of zinc supplements and polyunsaturated
fatty acids to treat acne is still in the experimental stages. A
true deficiency of these nutrients may cause sebaceous
glands to enlarge. We don't recommend self-therapy, however, especially with zinc, which is toxic in even moderate
doses.

DIETING

One-third of all teeenage girls are overweight, and most of
the other two-thirds *think* they are. That means that most
teens have a problem.

Teens who are really obese need help to reduce their weight or, if they're still growing, to maintain a steady weight as they grow taller. Those who aren't overweight, but think they are, need to develop a more realistic image of themselves. Otherwise they may waste their time (and health) on a series of fad diets that are not nutritionally balanced.

Why are teenage girls obsessed with weight? Perhaps because adolescence is the time that you are most conscious of your body. Also, in the very social and sometimes stressful world in which teens live, image is all-important. And the image that is held up to you (as well as to other age groups) is that of the very thin fashion model. Such an image is unrealistic—it's more like a male than a female form.

Females, after their adolescent growth spurt, have hips. Nature assumes that women will have children and that they will need the wider pelvic bone for child delivery. Until adolescence, boys and girls have about the same amount of body fat. But as they mature, boys gain more protein while girls gain some protein and more fat. That is natural, unless it becomes extreme or the girl resorts to drastic preventative measures.

For an overweight teenager, weight control is important and must be handled carefully.

It is believed that fat cells divide during adolescent growth. These cells will be with you for the rest of your life. If too many are produced, it will be even more difficult to reach and maintain a normal body weight when you're older.

You must choose a method of weight control carefully. Calorie restriction that is too severe can interfere with the normal growth process. Some doctors believe that children and teenagers should *not* try to lose weight, that instead they should develop a program to maintain their weight as they grow taller.

That's fine if you are only slightly overweight and are still growing taller. (Even a "holding pattern," however, requires planning, and we'll discuss this a little later.) But if you don't fit that description and seriously want to lose weight, consult your physician for a thorough evaluation, then ask the doctor to refer you to a dietitian, an "adolescent obesity" clinic, or some of the reputable self-help groups listed on page 164. Some have special groups for teenagers.

How can you know whether or not you're really overweight? Your own judgment may not be very valid, because most teenage girls think they're fat. One way to do a realistic evaluation is to compare your weight and height to the growth chart on page 28.

Remember, it's not what you weigh, but your weight in relation to your height that's important. For example, 125 lbs. (57 kg) would not be an excessive weight if you're 5'4" (163 cm) tall, but would if you're only 4'10" (147 cm) high. Check your height and weight against the chart. They may both be at the fifty percent level, which means that you're average for your age. Or they may both be at the ten percent or the ninety percent level. That means that you're either shorter or taller than average for your age.

Don't worry about that. Teenagers just grow at different rates at different times. If your weight fits your height, you're not overweight. But if your weight is at a higher percent line than your height, you're carrying a few extra pounds.

What can you do about that? We've mentioned two

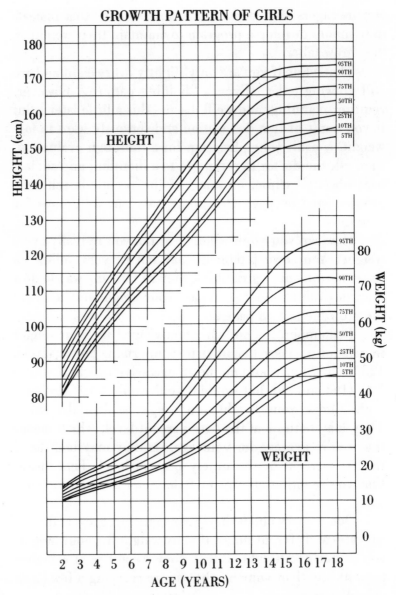

GROWTH PATTERN OF GIRLS

HEIGHT (cm)

WEIGHT (kg)

HEIGHT

WEIGHT

95TH
90TH
75TH
50TH
25TH
10TH
5TH

AGE (YEARS)

Adapted from Hamill, P.V.V., et al., *Amer. J. Clin. Nutr.* 32:607-629, 1979.

approaches—either lose weight or develop a "holding pattern." For example, Fran is thirteen years old, 4'10" (147 cm) tall, weighs 120 lbs. (55 kg) and is still growing. She should maintain her weight until her height catches up. Beth, on the other hand, weighs 140 lbs. (64 kg) at 5'4" (163 cm). She is eighteen years old and has already completed her basic growth. She needs to lose some weight. At her age, a rational low-energy diet will not be harmful.

There are many ways to approach weight loss or control. The methods we don't recommend are the fad diets currently popular (see page 159). They simply don't work. You may lose weight initially. (On a low-carbohydrate diet, most of the weight lost will be water.) But if you succeed in losing some fat, it rarely stays off for long, because such diets are not developed for your own life style. Most of us quickly return to our old eating habits.

There is no one weight program perfect for everyone, just as there is no one reason why some teenagers are overweight. Some may eat a lot, others may be very inactive. And there are many reasons for the overeating and underactivity. It may simply be due to improper habits developed from childhood that can be changed with serious and intelligent effort. In other instances, there are deep and sometimes unknown psychological reasons behind a weight problem. If our approach doesn't work, or if you can't bring yourself to try it, then consult a counselor, friend, or family doctor who can sympathize with your problem and either help you or refer you to appropriate help.

The basic approach to weight control is getting to know yourself. And isn't that what adolescence is all about? You'll have to do some serious self-evaluation. What do you eat? Where, when, and why do you eat? How do you exercise—or do you?

The details of this program are given in Chapter 7. Read it carefully. It's not the solution for everyone, but it's a good basic start. Get the help you need from reputable self-help groups or doctors, family, or friends. But remember, it's your decision and your responsibility to follow through.

ANOREXIA NERVOSA

The most extreme form of weight control is starvation; some teenagers as well as older women do resort to it. The body can tolerate a one- or two-day fast, but longer fasting periods should never be attempted except under complete and expert medical supervision, and only in the most extreme forms of overweight.

Despite this obvious logic, an estimated one in every 100 teenage girls in North America is starving. The equally sad point is that they have lost control of this starvation. They have anorexia nervosa.

Anorexia nervosa used to be a medical rarity, but now many hospitals maintain special wards for people with this condition. The word "anorexia" means a lack of appetite. "Nervosa" indicates a nerve condition. Neither definition gives an adequate description of the condition.

True anorexia nervosa is a condition found almost exclusively in women between twelve and twenty-five years of age. (A very few boys develop it, but usually at an earlier age. When boys have anorexia it almost entirely is due to severe psychological problems.) The cause of anorexia in adolescent girls and young women is not known. The symptoms are sometimes diverse, making diagnosis difficult; however, some symptoms appear to be common and are accepted by most physicians as criteria for anorexia.

After other illnesses, physical and psychological, are ruled out as a cause of severe weight loss, doctors evaluate other symptoms. Actual body weight, of course, is important. Anorexics weigh at least twenty-five percent less than normal. This low weight may be due to a great weight loss (usually fairly rapid) or to the fact that the girl did not gain weight normally as she was growing taller. Only fifteen to twenty percent of girls with anorexia nervosa were actually overweight to start with. But all of them "feel fat." This is a characteristic of many adolescent girls. No one knows why some go on to become anorexic while the others don't.

"Feeling fat" is only one of the distorted attitudes anorexic girls have about weight, eating, and themselves. A person of normal weight will underestimate her body size. An anorexic girl will consistently overestimate hers; her self-image is distorted. Even when she is only skin and bones, she will see herself as fat.

And as we said, she is usually not truly anorexic; i.e., without an appetite. She may be obsessed with food, nutrition, and diets. She may read all she can on these subjects. She may cook nutritious gourmet meals for the family (which she refuses to eat). She may go on eating binges, after which she feels guilty, forces herself to vomit the food, or exercises frantically in an attempt to use up the energy.

Amenorrhea (that is, no menstruation) is a common symptom. In some instances this occurs before other symptoms are apparent. This has led to the suggestion that anorexia nervosa is a hormonal problem. More often, amenorrhea occurs after a great deal of weight has been lost. There is a proved relationship between body weight and menstruation. Over the last 125 years, the average age at which menstruation starts has decreased from sixteen and one-half to twelve and one-half years. But younger girls are larger and heavier than they used to be, so the average weight at the start of menstruation has stayed the same. A certain body weight seems necessary to trigger hormonal changes that start the menstrual cycle. When a woman's weight drops below that weight for any reason— illness, fasting, or anorexia nervosa—menstruation will become irregular or stop altogether.

The possibility that hormonal disturbances exist in certain cases of anorexia nervosa cannot be entirely ruled out. But when these imbalances are identified it is impossible to know whether they cause anorexia or are caused *by* anorexia. Most experts believe that the latter is true.

Most of the current study and treatment of anorexia has emphasized the psychological nature of the disease. We have mentioned the distorted attitudes anorexics have towards their bodies and their eating habits. This distortion may extend to other sensations. They won't eat, despite their hunger, exercise violently though tired, and even deny that they are cold, although they have cold hands and feet, or that they are in pain. Anorexics may simply deny these realities.

Anorexics' denial of any external stimuli has been interpreted as an attempt to gain control over their lives. Studies have shown that many anorexics feel useless, highly dependent, and that others are controlling their lives. It has been suggested that they dread growing up and so try to suppress their growth and sexual maturation by self-imposed starvation.

Interestingly, anorexics most often come from upper- or upper middle-class families where there are high expectations for achievement. They are also likely to be overachievers. That is, they are A-students or good athletes, but they only have average abilities. Their achievements are due to excessive work.

The psychological symptoms of anorexia nervosa are so common that it may be possible to use them to identify preanorexics. These are people having the psychological problems but not the full-blown disease.

Watch for:

- a dramatic weight loss
- an obsession with nutrition and fad diets (only eating lettuce and yoghurt, for example)
- a sudden interest in food preparation and clean-up, but not in eating
- eating binges followed by self-induced vomiting or use of laxatives
- withdrawal from family and friends
- a delay in starting menstruation, or menstruation ceasing
- a noticeable mood swing or deep depression
- a lack of concern about problems
- a delusion about appearance
- a determination not to eat when hungry, or to rest when tired
- an obsession with strenuous exercise
- endless studying, desperation for good grades
- difficulty in concentrating or in sleeping

These signs are not intended to be used as an absolute diagnosis of anorexia nervosa, but could help to identify someone who is developing the condition. Most anorexics do not recognize their condition. They also attempt to isolate themselves from family and friends. Therefore, family, friends, and also health professionals must be aware of the symptoms and insist that the anorexic girl get the professional help she needs. And professional help is needed; for ten to fifteen percent of anorexics, the condition is fatal.

TEENAGE MOTHERS

In the United States one-third of all girls between fifteen and twenty years of age have or will have at least one unwanted pregnancy. Forty thousand teenagers in Canada had babies in 1978. Approximately another sixty thousand had legal abortions. These numbers are growing and the current epidemic of teenage pregnancies is a hotly debated issue among sociologists.

An early unplanned pregnancy usually causes numerous crises for a teenager: psychological, social, nutritional, and sometimes economic crises. If she decides to continue the pregnancy, she may have to drop out of school, isolate herself from her family and friends, and in many cases have to live on public assistance. The younger the girl, the more serious the consequences.

The special needs of pregnant teenage mothers are being recognized and met sometimes through such programs as Teen Age Program in Santa Ana, California, or the St. Paul Maternal and Infant Care Project. These services include extensive nutritional counseling for teenage girls along with other necessary education. Unfortunately, there aren't enough of these services yet to meet the need. Too many girls receive little education, support, or help. All too often, the help they do get may be from ill-informed people who only perpetuate myths and misunderstandings about pregnancy.

Teenage pregnancies are classed as "high-risk." The

adolescent girl is more likely to have complications than is a woman of twenty to thirty-five years of age. These complications can include toxemia (see page 52) and iron-deficiency anemia. Her baby is also more likely to be premature and underweight, both of which conditions put the newborn baby at risk.

During pregnancy, the teenage girl is still growing. Her nutritional needs are already high, and become even higher with pregnancy. But the usual diets of most pregnant teens will not supply these nutrients. Like many other teenagers, she may use a limited variety of foods, rely heavily on low-nutrient snack foods, eat irregularly, and have a poor knowledge of foods and nutrition. The added stress of the pregnancy may affect her diet even further.

Following birth, the baby may still be in danger. Because of today's trend towards small families, girls do not learn about feeding and caring for children as they once did. Special efforts are needed to prepare for this role.

How can you avoid these mistakes? First, check programs in your area geared towards the pregnant teen. Then, learn all you can about pregnancy (see Chapter 3). And finally, as quickly as possible after you discover you are pregnant, get started on a healthy diet. Whether or not you've made a decision about your future, look after yourself and your baby *now*.

 Eating Strategy   *Pregnant Teen*

FOOD	SERVINGS/DAY	NUTRIENTS
Milk (vita-mins A- and	4-8 oz. (250 mL) glasses (or equiva-	All of calcium, vita-min D and riboflavin

(Chart continues)

FOOD	SERVINGS/DAY	NUTRIENTS
D-fortified; if calories are a problem use skim milk or milk products)	lent in cheese, ice cream, etc.)	needed; about ½ of needed protein, vitamin A and niacin and ⅓ of needed thiamin
Meat	2-3 oz. (90 g) servings	protein, B vitamins, iron, trace minerals
Egg	1	protein, iron, vitamin A
Fruit	at least 2, one citrus, preferably raw, or citrus vitamin C-fortified *juice* (not drink)	vitamin C, folate
Vegetables	2-3 servings of dark green and/or yellow	vitamin A, folate, vitamin C, fiber
Bread and Cereals	3-4 servings	B vitamins, iron and other minerals, fiber
Additional breads and cereals, vegetables, starch foods such as corn, rice or potatoes		to make up any extra calories needed

Of course, this eating plan can be individualized to include the specific foods you like, but try to include a great variety of foods. Mothers-to-be are sometimes more motivated to eat when they realize they are eating for the baby. (In some programs for pregnant teenagers, mothers are asked to write "For Baby" on the quart of milk they're to drink each day.) The snacking does not have to be eliminated. Again, it's not the snack, but the type of snack that is important. Nutritious snacks from any of the basic food groups can be incorporated into the total diet.

All the nutrients required by a pregnant teen can be obtained from the diet. However, this is the one case where we might bend our general rule against supplements and recommend a good multivitamin-mineral supplement with folate. The composition of that supplement should be close to the one given in the table on page 199.

Three of four unwed teenage mothers are now keeping their babies. If the mothers are poorly nourished, the deficiencies will be perpetuated in their children. Good teen pregnancy programs include discussions of breast-feeding, bottle-feeding, weaning, and nourishing children. We've discussed most of these topics in Chapters 3 and 4.

ADOLESCENTS, ALCOHOL, AND CIGARETTES

Too often these days a desire to grow up, to be independent, is expressed by the early use of alcohol and cigarettes.

Tobacco is unhealthy. Its relationship to lung cancer has been proved. And its effect in destroying vitamin C is also well known. Sensible alcohol use, on the other hand, is not particularly unhealthy. (By sensible, we mean one beer or one glass of wine occasionally, not a weekly bash.) Alcohol does make special demands on nutrients, though, and while these are moderate (with moderate alcohol intake), be sure to get all your nutrients through a balanced diet. Remember that calories from alcohol do count (seven calories per gram of pure alcohol or 150 calories per bottle of regular beer).

A HEAD START

Your current eating habits are very important to your present health, appearance, and performance. But please take one minute to consider that they are also essential to the rest of your life.

What you ate as a child is certainly important, but the way you choose to eat while you're in your late teens often determines how you'll eat as an adult. Those habits of overeating, undereating, or poor eating will be much harder to change later.

Fat cells you develop in your teen years stay with you. If you stay overweight, you're more likely to have diabetes and high blood pressure in adulthood. Both of these conditions are risk factors for heart disease. Many of the diseases, in fact, that plague the current adult population—diabetes, heart disease, high blood pressure—have their beginnings in our young years, and these diseases are believed to be related to diet.

If there is any history of diabetes, heart problems, or stroke in your family, you should have a periodic thorough checkup, including a test of your blood fats (cholesterol and triglycerides). If these are high, you'll be prescribed a diet that is low in fat, particularly in saturated fats.

Even if you seem to have no problems at the moment, we suggest you start learning to eat the sensible way—less fat, saturated fat, cholesterol, salt, and sugar. There's no proof yet that this will protect you from heart disease later in your life, but it's a good diet that will contain fewer calories. Someday we may find that it actually helps.

3 The Mother-Woman

When you become pregnant, whether the pregnancy was planned or unplanned, you'll soon realize that you and your life will never be the same again. Mothering begins long before your baby's birth.

Many women only first develop a serious interest in nutrition during their first pregnancy. That's really a bit late. The old adage is that you need to start preparing for pregnancy—nutritionally—at least two years before you become pregnant. A woman with good nutrient stores at the start of her pregnancy will be better able to nourish her child before its birth.

Most women don't realize that they're pregnant until

they've missed at least one menstrual period. That means that they've already been pregnant for about six weeks, and much has already happened in that time. By the seventh to eighth week of pregnancy, your baby weighs thirty grams, or one ounce. It is now called a fetus and is identifiably human. This early life of the baby is critical because this is the time when abnormalities are established. In humans, most congenital defects are established by the tenth week, and most natural abortions prior to twelve weeks are of abnormal fetuses. Fortunately, the amounts of nutrients required for the first seven weeks of fetal development are so small that it is next to impossible (short of a very long starvation) for enough not to be available from either the mother's diet or her body stores.

An established routine of healthy eating is important at this point, not because it can prevent such abnormalities but because it helps develop the nutrient stores that will be needed later in the pregnancy.

Your unborn baby grows rapidly. At three months, the sex of the child is established; blood is being formed. The face becomes visible at four months, and scalp hair appears. By five months, you can hear the heart beat (with a stethoscope); nails and even enamel on the baby's teeth, which are still embedded in its gums, have formed. Eyebrows and eyelashes form by six months, and bone mineralization begins.

Up until about the eighth month of pregnancy, the growth and development has involved mainly organs, muscles, and bones. The baby has very little fat. If a child is born prematurely at this stage, it resembles a wrinkled prune: there is no fat under the skin. Over the next month, fourteen grams of fat are formed every day, the wrinkles smooth out, all the vital organs are developed—and this new person is ready to join the outside world.

In a short nine months, a single cell (a fertilized egg) has grown to a baby weighing from six to eight pounds, a six-billion-fold weight increase! That represents a lot of energy and nutrients that must be supplied by the mother — most of which will be needed during the last six months of pregnancy.

NOURISHING YOU AND YOUR BABY

By the end of the third month, the placenta and its blood supply are fully established. Essentially all of the baby's nourishment is transferred from your blood to the baby's blood in the placenta. It then travels down the blood vessel in the umbilical cord to the baby.

Three factors determine the amount of nutrients the baby will get:

- the rate of the blood flow of the mother
- the amount of nutrients in the mother's blood
- the transfer of nutrients to the baby's blood in the placenta

During pregnancy, a woman's blood flow naturally increases, although in rare cases disease of the heart or blood vessel system may limit the supply of nutrients. It is obvious, then, that the baby's growth is dependent on its mother's health. The nutrients in the mother's blood will come from either her diet or her body stores. These should be high enough to ensure that adequate amounts reach the baby. Nature ensures that increases in body hormones (estrogen and progesterone) help your body retain protein and metabolize fat, so a good supply of glucose and amino acids will be available to the baby.

A baby is not a complete parasite, but some nutrients

are transferred to the baby at your expense. These include iron, calcium, magnesium, zinc, pyridoxine (vitamin B_6), vitamin C, amino acids, and folic acid. That's why iron deficiency anemia is often a problem in pregnancy. Also, your bone calcium may decrease if your diet is not supplying the baby's needs. The baby must compete with you for such other nutrients as thiamin and riboflavin. If your blood is low in these, your baby's will be too.

What's happening to the baby is fascinating. But let's look at what's happening to *you*.

The baby itself accounts for only about one-third of the total weight you'll gain during pregnancy. The rest of the weight is the placenta, the amniotic fluid (the water the baby floats in), and your own additional body water, fat and breast and uterus tissue. In addition, the total amount of blood you have increases by almost one-third to ensure delivery of nutrients to the baby and removal of its waste materials—such as urea and carbon dioxide.

Do not be concerned about water retention unless you are showing signs of toxemia, a condition we'll discuss more fully later. Also, fat storage is natural. It will be used in one of two ways: as a safety store for later in the pregnancy, or in preparation for lactation. (It seems the human body has not yet learned that all women don't breast-feed their babies, and it readies itself nevertheless).

Weight gain isn't the only thing that's happening. The activity of your stomach and intestines slows down so that food takes longer to pass through. While this increases the absorption of all nutrients, it also may cause nausea and constipation. Constipation is a greater problem late in pregnancy, when the enlarged uterus presses against the large intestine. Absorption of such critical nutrients as iron and calcium increases. This happens despite the fact that there is less acid in your stomach. (Stomach acid usually favors the absorption of minerals.) Total blood flow increases, and the activity of your kidneys increases by as much as sixty percent. In late pregnancy, your enlarged uterus presses against your bladder. These changes increase the need to urinate.

The concentration of nutrients and other substances in the blood changes. Some are increased; for example, carotene, vitamin E, cholesterol, and other fats. Others, such as protein, vitamin A, vitamin C, hemoglobin, and red blood cells, decrease. But part of that decrease is because total blood water increases. So slightly low hemoglobin levels do not indicate real anemia at this stage.

In the light of all of these physical changes, you can see how important it is to take care of yourself. Your diet has to be adequate for the baby, for you, and for the new tissue you'll develop over this nine months.

One critical aspect of pregnancy is weight gain, a controversial topic for many years. Pregnant women who are overweight at the start of their pregnancy, or who have a large weight gain during pregnancy, are more likely to have stillborn infants and to develop toxemia. The extra weight is an added strain to the back and leg muscles and may be hard to take off after the pregnancy.

Pregnancy is *not*, however, the time to try to lose weight. The fetus needs a continual supply of blood sugar (glucose) for energy. If your energy intake is very low, your blood glucose drops and fatty acids and substances called ketone bodies build up in your blood. Your tissues can use these for energy, but it's not known how well the baby can. Premature babies or babies with a low birth weight can be the result if you gain too little weight during the pregnancy (or if you begin the pregnancy unusually underweight.) Don't take risks. If you want to lose weight, do it before or after your pregnancy—not during. A sensible weight gain is essential.

How much weight *should* you gain? For many years, it has been fashionable to recommend that women gain only about fifteen pounds (7 kg), essentially the weight of the placenta, the uterus, the amniotic fluid, and a small baby. This practice started in the 1800s when many women had deformed pelvises, caused by rickets (a condition related to vitamin D deficiency). If the baby was small, delivery wasn't such a risk to either mother or baby. Fortunately, rickets is a thing of the past in most developed countries. And the practice of severely restricting weight gains during pregnancy should be too. A gain of twenty to thirty pounds (9 to 14 kg) is now recommended.

You need only consume about 200 to 300 extra calories a day after the first three months of pregnancy to gain this weight. Your goal should be a smooth and consistent weight gain—a sudden gain will probably be due to water accumulation. This must be dealt with by moderate salt (sodium) restriction or, in extreme conditions, diuretics or other drugs prescribed by your doctor.

A normal weight gain would be: one to three months, little or none; four to seven months, one-half to three-quarters of a pound a week; and seven to nine months, three-quarters to one pound a week. You may not gain any weight during the last few weeks of pregnancy.

The old saying that you are eating for two is true, but remember, one of the two is very small. Your total energy intake should not double, but be only ten to fifteen percent greater than when you weren't pregnant.

Your increased energy need is actually less than your increased need for other nutrients. The extra need for other nutrients varies anywhere from fifteen percent for niacin to 100 percent for folic acid and vitamin D.

Let's assume that your diet right now is that of the average nutrition-conscious woman. You know about the value of milk products, fresh fruits and vegetables, and whole grain cereals. Now you're pregnant. What more do you need to do?

Your body's—your baby's—demand for increased nutrients calls for a careful, more selective balance of proper foods. Knowing the nutrients you need and how to obtain them means that you can perform that juggling act like an expert.

PREGNANCY AND KEY NUTRIENTS

The nutrients that are needed in the largest additional amounts during pregnancy are protein, folic acid, vitamin B_{12}, iron, calcium, and vitamin D. When you consider the changes that are taking place in you and your child, this makes a lot of sense.

Extra *protein* is required for the growth of all the components—the baby, of course, and the placenta, breast and uterine tissue, and blood proteins. Pregnancy and lactation are the periods of your life when you need more protein than a man. If you don't get enough protein, your baby will likely be smaller than normal. You yourself may suffer from anemia, poor muscle tone, low resistance to infection, and possibly a decreased ability to produce milk.

In North America, women normally get enough protein during their pregnancy. The average intake is generally greater than the recommended intake. The only women for whom inadequate protein may be a problem are those who cannot afford to buy the proper food, or who follow some rather off-beat diet. For example, on a very severe reducing diet, the protein available will be used primarily for energy rather than growth. Also, a pure vegetarian diet (no meat, fish, milk, or eggs) may not have the adequate amounts or appropriate types of protein unless it is wisely balanced (see page 169 for a discussion of vegetarian diets).

Remember that while protein is important, even essential, amounts exceeding the protein requirements will simply be used for energy; you will end up storing this energy as extra fat, your baby won't.

Folic acid, vitamin B_{12}, and iron are all essential for producing blood in the baby and for the extra amount of blood you yourself develop and maintain. During pregnancy, folic acid excretion is increased, and its absorption is decreased. This means that you need extra amounts of this nutrient in your diet. Symptoms of folate deficiency (macrocytic or megaloblastic anemia) appear in some women during their pregnancy.

Folic acid comes from the word foliage; therefore, most green leafy vegetables, especially asparagus, green beans, spinach, brussel sprouts, cabbage, and broccoli are good sources, along with cantaloupe, kidney, liver, orange juice, soybeans, wheat bran, and wheat germ. Include at least one serving of one of these each day. Even a daily folate supplement may be advisable. This should contain not more than 400 mg of folate, as large amounts sometimes mask another type of anemia caused by a deficiency of vitamin B_{12}.

Vitamin B_{12} is found in a great variety of foods — meat, milk, eggs, fish, and poultry. Deficiencies are rare except in long-term "pure" vegetarians (i.e., vegetarians whose diet excludes all those foods). A special type of anemia, called pernicious anemia, is caused by a decrease in the absorption of B_{12}. Vitamin B_{12} injections are needed rather than vitamin supplements.

Finally, the big problem for all women — *iron*. Iron is necessary for that increased blood volume and for ensuring that both you and your baby have adequate supplies of iron in your livers. Fortunately, iron absorption increases four-fold during pregnancy, so any iron in the diet is better used. Iron is one nutrient for which the baby has first claim. It will be moved to the baby's blood at the mother's expense.

There is some controversy about exactly how much iron is needed. The Canadian Recommended Daily Nutrient Intake recommends only an additional one milligram per day, but this is assuming that you already have adequate iron stores at the beginning of the pregnancy. Don't assume that.

In the United States, the Recommended Daily Allowances do not even list an additional intake of iron, but state that "the increased requirement during pregnancy cannot be met by the iron content of habitual American diets nor by the existing iron stores of many women; therefore, the use of 30 to 60 mg of supplemental iron is recommended."

Don't rely on the supplement entirely, but use one or more of the "iron-rich foods" every day. Take a supplement of thirty to sixty milligrams of iron each day. The best type is ferrous sulfate, which is easily absorbed. Iron supplements cause constipation in some women. This is easily overcome by increasing fiber intake and by cutting down on the amount of iron used each day—if there has been no indication of anemia at regular medical checkups.

FOOD SOURCES OF IRON

FOOD	MG/AVERAGE SERVING	RATING
Calf or lamb liver	9.6	Excellent
Beef or chicken liver	5.2	Very Good
Beef, lamb, pork, or veal	2.7	Good
Beans, baked with molasses	2.3	Good
Lima beans, prunes	1.8	Fair
Bread, enriched or whole grain (3 slices)	1.7	Fair
Chicken or turkey	1.6	Fair
Peas, fresh or frozen	1.5	Fair
Cereals, enriched or whole grain	1.3	Fair
Egg, 1 whole	1.1	Fair

At about the fifth month of pregnancy, *calcium* starts to be deposited in the baby's bones. To do this, the baby uses the total calcium in your blood every twenty hours. This, of course, has to be replaced by calcium either from your diet or your bones—and calcium taken from the diet would be better. As *vitamin D* is essential for the absorption of calcium, both nutrients are needed in extra amounts. This may benefit your baby more than you! One study found that a high calcium intake caused babies, but not their mothers, to have harder bones.

There may, however, be an obvious benefit for you. Leg and back cramps and general leg weakness are unpleasant side effects of pregnancy. This can often be relieved with a good calcium intake—from either your diet or from supplements.

Use a lot of milk products—the equivalent of three to four glasses of milk a day. If you're not able to do this, or still find you have cramps and weakness, use a calcium supplement—up to 600 mg of elemental calcium a day. Most multivitamin-mineral pills have very little calcium, so you'll have to look to either calcium lactate or calcium gluconate pills.

The need for most other nutrients also increases, but not as dramatically. *Thiamin, riboflavin,* and *niacin* are necessary for energy utilization and tissue growth. *Pyridoxine* (vitamin B_6) is needed to use protein properly. *Vitamin C* is used in the formation of connective tissue; very low intakes have led to the rupture of fetal membranes. It is also necessary to convert folic acid to the active form in the body necessary for its function in blood formation and cell growth.

Vitamin A is necessary for the formation of all epithelial tissue (for example, skin, lining of the stomach). A good intake also ensures that your baby and you will have good liver stores. Your stored vitamin A can later be transferred to your baby through your milk. A good diet already includes all of these nutrients, so no extra effort is needed on your part.

Despite the fact that the scientific name of *vitamin E,* tocopherol, means "to bear child," the significance of vitamin E in human pregnancy is still not known. Very little of the vitamin E in the blood crosses to the baby. There is no indication that women cannot have normal pregnancies on the usual amount of vitamin E in the diet; large supplemental doses are definitely not required.

 Eating Strategy *Pregnancy*

Select basic foods to ensure an adequate intake of all nutrients with only enough calories for optimal weight gain. Small, frequent meals may help prevent nausea, heartburn, and hunger pangs. They also keep your blood glucose level up so you won't become weak. Foods high in fiber should be used to help prevent constipation. If your legs and ankles swell, you may cut out salt added at the table or in cooking and highly salted foods such as bacon, pickles, and some snacks. Even though milk does contain sodium, don't cut it from your diet.

A good diet should include the following:

FOOD	AMOUNT	NUTRIENTS
Milk, whole or 2%	3-4 8 oz. (250 mL) glasses a day (or equivalent in cheese or other milk products)	protein, calcium, vitamin D and riboflavin; vitamin A (in whole or fortified milk)
Meat, lean, poultry, fish	2-4 oz. (60-120 g) servings a day	protein, B vitamins iron, other minerals
Eggs	3-4 per week	protein, iron, vitamin A
Dark green leafy vegetables (occasionally raw)	1-2 servings a day	folic acid, fiber, vitamin A, and vitamin C
Other vegetables cooked or raw	2-3 servings a day	vitamin A, fiber
Fruit	1 citrus fruit or juices with added vitamin C; others as wanted	vitamin C, folic acid
Whole grain breads and cereals	3-4 servings	protein, B vitamins, minerals, fiber

Morning sickness is a common complaint during early pregnancy. If you suffer from this problem, try small, frequent meals or foods such as melba toast, crackers, or baked potatoes. Eat crackers before you get out of bed if the morning is your worst time. (Morning sickness can occur at any time of the day.) Fortunately for most women, this unpleasant side effect of pregnancy is short-lived and disappears by itself. If it persists and you vomit excessively, you'll lose a lot of protein and minerals. Your doctor may therefore prescribe a low-fat, dry diet for a while.

There are antinausea drugs available, but some reports show that these might cause abnormalities in babies. This has not been absolutely proved, and the drugs are allowed on the market. It would be best, however, to avoid them if at all possible, especially during the early part of your pregnancy. If you feel you need this type of help, check with your doctor.

EXTRA VITAMINS AND MINERALS?

We've recommended supplements of iron, folic acid, and calcium for pregnant women. But other supplements are generally not necessary if you follow the basic eating strategy.

The Diet Dispensary in Montreal, Quebec, has been successful with a program that aimed to help a group of women produce healthy, normal babies; previously their babies had been underweight at birth. The magic supplement? One quart (or 1 L) of milk and one orange a day.

If you use supplements, they should be just that— supplements, not a replacement for a balanced diet. Food contains a variety of trace nutrients that will likely not be in supplements—and probably shouldn't be because safe dosages are not known. Pregnancy definitely isn't the time to use massive doses of vitamins either. At best, they're a waste of money; at worst, they can injure the baby.

It's been known for some time that if a woman takes large doses of vitamin C (500 mg or more a day), this vitamin is readily transferred to the baby. The baby becomes dependent on these large doses. After birth, it will develop vitamin C deficiency unless it's given vitamin C in amounts larger than are generally necessary.

Vitamin A is an even greater problem. It is quite toxic. Overdoses (35,000-150,000 I.U./day) have caused abnormalities in the kidney, urinary tract, and nerves of human infants.

If you're using milk products fortified with vitamin D, you should not use a vitamin D supplement. Excess vitamin D may lead to abnormal calcium deposits in the baby.

TOXEMIA IN PREGNANCY

Few people realize that toxemia is the major cause of death in pregnant women in North America. The condition is complex, and the symptoms include loss of protein in the urine, retention of water, face "puffiness," loss of appetite, and high blood pressure.

The exact cause of toxemia is not known, but it occurs more often among poorer women. It may also be brought on by fasting. Women who are overweight or who gain a lot of weight during their pregnancy are also more likely to develop toxemia.

Traditionally, treatment consisted of severely restricting salt (sodium) intake to control fluid retention and high blood pressure. The treatment wasn't extremely successful, however, probably because toxemia involves more than simply too much salt. Some studies indicate that women who are generally not well nourished are more likely to develop toxemia: overall diet *is* important.

A little water retention is normal during pregnancy. If your ankles and legs start to swell, try not to stand up, or stand still too long (walking and exercise may help move the water out). Whenever you can, put your feet up. You can also cut your salt intake slightly by substituting herbs and spices for salt in foods, and by limiting the amounts of such foods as bacon, pickles, and salted snack foods. Sudden weight gain, face puffiness, or blurred vision should be reported to your doctor immediately.

PROTECTING THE BABY

We've emphasized the transfer of nutrients to your baby from you. But other substances can travel this route as well: drugs, pollutants such as lead, even nicotine and alcohol.

Cigarette smoking and social drinking are a way of life for many people. But your unborn baby is vulnerable, and you may have to change your life style—at least temporarily.

If ever there was a good time for giving up (or at least cutting down on) smoking, pregnancy is that time. Smoking cigarettes affects two nutrients essential for your baby's growth—vitamin C and oxygen. Because of changes in the intestine caused by smoking, a large part of the vitamin C is destroyed before it can be absorbed. Smoking also increases the level of carboxyhemoglobin in your blood and lowers the amount of oxygen-carrying hemoglobin. It is believed that this is the main reason that smoking women generally have smaller babies and more premature deliveries, abortions, stillbirths, and neonatal deaths than women who do not smoke.

Smoking marijuana, though common, is not a great idea either. Some studies indicate that babies of mothers who use a lot of marijuana show some damage to their chromosomes (genetic material). It is not known what actual effect this may have on the child, but why take chances?

The other popular social drug is alcohol, and it too may affect your pregnancy. Long ago Aristotle warned that women who drank heavily had abnormal babies. This fact has just recently been rediscovered.

The extreme result of misuse of alcohol during pregnancy is called fetal alcohol syndrome. Babies with this condition are born small, grow and develop slowly, and have unusual faces. Possibly a third or more of the babies of women who drink heavily will have this condition. Many children of women who drink less heavily have one or more of the symptoms of fetal alcohol syndrome. One study showed women who only had a few drinks a week had babies who had sleeping difficulties.

But what about a "social" drinker? No one knows how much alcohol is "safe." Therefore the best plan would be to use alcohol very rarely, if at all, during your pregnancy.

Other drugs and pregnancy don't mix either. The classic case is thalidomide. This drug was in use for four years before its severe effect was appreciated. No drug has proved to be as harmful as thalidomide. A number of prescription and nonprescription drugs, however, if used in very large amounts, are potentially teratogenic (have the ability to produce malformed infants). These include Aminopterin, desamphetamine, and excess antacids, ninotinamide, and iron. Even normal doses of aspirin during the last two weeks of pregnancy can slightly change some blood clotting factors and platelet functions in the baby. A general rule is to take only absolutely necessary prescription drugs during pregnancy, and those at the lowest doses possible.

FEEDING YOUR NEWBORN BABY

While you're thinking about feeding yourself and your unborn child, you should begin to give some thought to what you'll feed the baby after it is born. Now is the time to plan how to nourish the new baby.

First, decide whether you'll breast- or bottle-feed. This is a big decision and one that you should make early in pregnancy. You'll have to make preparations. If you opt for bottle-feeding, you'll need bottles, nipples, some means of sterilizing the bottles, and of course, the formula itself.

Preparations also have to be made for breast-feeding, but of a different kind. While breast-feeding is a natural way of feeding, it doesn't come naturally to many women in North America. Breast-feeding has only come into fashion once more in the last decade, so that we are relearning an old, old skill.

Before we get to the hows, let's discuss some of the pros and cons of breast- versus bottle-feeding. What you want to choose for your baby is the ideal baby food—or as nearly ideal a food as possible. This food should be easy to use, inexpensive, nutritionally adequate, contain beneficial substances other than nutrients, but no harmful materials.

Breast milk is perfect. It answers all of these needs and is the original convenience food—ready to use, preheated, and with a unique supply and demand feature: the more the baby drinks, the more milk the breast produces.

(We will look more closely at its nutritional advantages later.) Despite this fact, millions of women choose not to breast-feed.

Many years ago a woman who didn't breast-feed had two choices: to use formulas that were anything but nutritionally adequate, or to obtain a wet nurse. As late as 1910, a Directory of Wet Nurses was maintained in the United States. Often, though, even these breast-fed infants didn't fare well as wet nurses tried to suckle as many infants as they could in order to make more money.

Many women in North America have felt that breast-feeding was inconvenient, and the practice declined progressively until about 1970. At that time, only twenty-five percent of all babies were totally breast-fed at one week of age. Even fewer got breast milk as they got older.

Many factors may have influenced this decline, but primarily those of status and social pressure. Breast-feeding (particularly in public) has not been socially acceptable. In a world full of nudity in fashion, in films, in art, breast-feeding was considered obscene. (How irrational we humans are at times.) More practical problems also discouraged the practice; for instance, women's clothes were not made to accommodate feeding their babies.

The unacceptability of breast-feeding even permeated the medical profession, and it must accept considerable responsibility for the decline. Recent medical education included information about bottle-feeding and essentially nothing about breast-feeding. Horror stories of women being given drugs to dry up their milk without their knowledge or consent were not rare. More commonly, doctors simply advised the new mother to bottle-feed her infant and this became the trend.

We're glad to say that this has changed—finally. The

Commentary on Breast-Feeding, issued jointly by the American Academy of Pediatrics and the Canadian Pediatric Society, states that "most full-term infants should be breast-fed."

The Nutrition Committee of the Canadian Pediatric Society has much more strongly advocated breast-feeding. Its goal: to double the number of babies still being breast-fed at two months of age. In cooperation with Health and Welfare Canada and the La Leche League, it has produced an information packet for all health professionals (particularly doctors) to help achieve this goal.

You have to make the decision, weighing the pros and cons. Breast-feeding means you are totally responsible for feeding your baby. Depending on your viewpoint, this can be either good or bad. Many women who have breast-fed remember this as one of the most satisfying experiences of their lives. Your baby will feel secure and loved if you breast-feed—and if you are enjoying it.

Babies who are bottle-fed also feel this security if they are held while fed and not given a propped-up bottle. Bottle-feeding offers the whole family the opportunity to be actively involved with the baby. And, as we will see, modern formulas are a remarkably good substitute for breast milk.

Whatever method you choose, make sure it's *your* decision, not your doctor's, your neighbour's, or your aunt's. If you breast-feed, other members of the family may either be happy to let you take over, or may feel that they are being left out. If they do want to be involved with the care of the new baby, ask them to help with such things as bathing and dressing the baby.

There are other considerations to bear in mind. Social activities are made slightly more complicated when a hungry baby begins to wail for the breast. You may not appreciate beating a hasty retreat to a restroom for a long feeding session, and public breast-feeding frequently causes some raised eyebrows. But many of today's clothing styles often make it possible to breast-feed in public without anyone knowing — not that anyone should be offended. Shawls or baby blankets can also offer a clever camouflage.

The major inconvenience will likely come as you move back into your normal social or work life. We are not as progressive in North America as in some countries where breast-feeding is considered the natural thing to do. Here, employers do not maintain nurseries where women can go to take care of their babies. But there have been a few highly publicized cases of women suing in order to bring their babies to work. These cases are being won by the mothers — and the babies.

For some mothers, the most convenient arrangement is to stay home several months after the birth. Too few maternity leaves allow for that; some may be only a few weeks long. In cases of more generous leaves, only part of the salary is covered and/or there is no guarantee that your exact position will be available when you want to return to work.

Perhaps in the future we will follow Sweden's example, allowing *both* parents several months maternity leave. In Sweden the parent — mother or father — caring for the baby is granted leave. In North America it will take a lot of hard negotiating by more women (unfortunately, often through male-dominated unions) who demand sufficient time to care for their infants without being penalized for having given birth.

Another economic question is the actual cost of breast milk *vs.* formula. Most studies show that there is little or no difference between the cost of adequately feeding the mother to produce milk and buying formula. But the cost of bottles, sterilizer, or convenience items like disposable nursers is extra.

BREAST MILK vs. SUBSTITUTES

Naturally, you want to see that your baby gets the best food possible, all the nutrients needed to grow and develop normally. Let's compare breast milk with cow's milk and with formulas.

Your first breast secretion is not mature human milk but colostrum. When you first see this thin yellowish fluid, you may doubt that you'll ever be able to feed your baby. But take heart. Colostrum is a unique fluid especially designed for young babies. It has less fat and lactose (milk sugar) than mature milk but more protein, which is what your baby needs for early, very fast growth. Also, the protein consists mostly of whey proteins rather than casein. Whey protein is more readily digested and less likely to cause tummy upset.

Over three to four weeks, the colostrum will change to mature milk. This milk is still different than cow's milk. It has less protein and total minerals. These differences are again important for your baby.

You may not think that less is better, but in this case it is. Your baby is not growing quite as rapidly now. Also, a young baby is still not mature in many ways. For example, the baby's kidneys cannot yet reabsorb water properly to concentrate the urine. That means that anything that is excreted in the urine, particularly minerals and protein breakdown products such as urea, will cause a lot of water to be lost. If your baby is fed a milk or formula with too much protein and minerals, so much water may be lost that dehydration results.

Skim cow's milk is usually the protein source in formulas (Emfamil or Enfalac and Similac are some common brands), and may be supplemented with demineralized whey (SMA) or soy protein (Similac Advance). For babies who are allergic to cow's milk, special formulas based on soy products are available (Isomil, Neo-Mull-Soy, ProSobee, Nursoy, Sobee, Mull-Soy, for example). Whatever the protein source, the total protein content of the formulas is similar to that of breast milk. Also a lot of minerals have been removed from these formulas.

Despite all the advances made in infant formulas, breast milk still has some basic advantages. Human milk contains more whey protein, which is more easily digested. Also, the amino acids in the proteins of human milk may be uniquely suited to the infant. The liver of the baby, particularly a premature one, is not very efficient in converting one amino acid, methionine, to another one, cysteine. Therefore, extra amounts of cysteine, found in breast milk, help in growth. Also, the baby's liver cannot easily metabolize the amino acid tyrosine, which happens to be low in breast milk. If the baby gets too much tyrosine, it will accumulate in the blood, and a condition called neonatal tyrosinemia will result. This is not a serious problem unless blood tyrosine levels are very high, and usually only happens if the baby is very premature or is not getting enough vitamin C.

When your baby is born, its bones are quite soft. During the first few months of life, minerals, particularly calcium, are deposited in your baby's bones to strengthen them enough to support her weight when she starts to walk. So don't attempt to force your child to start to walk early.

The calcium to phosphorus ratio is 2.2 to 1 in breast milk and about 1.3 to 1 in cow's milk and most formulas. The higher ratio helps the absorption of calcium.

Fats in human milk are better absorbed than those in cow's milk because of the difference in their fatty acid composition. In addition, human milk contains an enzyme that partly digests the fat. The absorption of the fat from the vegetable oils used in most infant formula is now nearly as good as the fat of breast milk.

Fat in breast milk is one of the factors that can be changed by what you're eating. Over the past years, breast milk has become progressively more polyunsaturated as the consumption of vegetable oils and polyunsaturated margarines has increased. The amount of fat and energy in human milk also increases throughout each nursing period. Some suggest that the higher calorie (energy) value of the later milk helps the baby feel fuller and prevents her from drinking too much.

The sugar *lactose* is called milk sugar because it only occurs naturally in milk. Cow's milk and some formulas also contain lactose. Lactose is important for two reasons. One—it favors the growth of specific bacteria in the baby's intestine. These "friendly" bacteria inhibit the growth of some not so friendly microorganisms. Also, lactose is not as sweet-tasting as table sugar (sucrose), so a baby may not be as likely to develop a sweet tooth.

But lactose produces tooth decay just the same way other sugars do. So when your baby begins to develop teeth, she should not be propped up with a bottle, particularly if she's going to sleep. After she's had her bottle, rinse her mouth out with water. Otherwise she may develop what's known as the nursing bottle syndrome—decay of the top and bottom front teeth.

Lactose intolerance—the inability to digest lactose—

COMPARISON OF COLOSTRUM (EARLY MILK), MATURE MILK,
COW'S MILK, AND FORMULA

	COLOSTRUM	MATURE BREAST MILK	COW'S MILK	FORMULA
ENERGY	Moderate	Moderately Low	High	Moderately Low
PROTEIN	High	Moderately Low Mainly Whey (Unique Composition)	High Mainly Casein	Moderately Low Skim Cow's Milk Whey and/or Soy Protein
FAT	Low	See p. 61	Butter Fat	Vegetable Oils
CARBOHYDRATES	Low, Lactose	Lactose	Lactose	Lactose Corn Syrup Solids and/or Sucrose
MINERALS	High	Low	High	Varies, may be low
CALCIUM TO PHOSPHORUS RATIO	High	High	Low	Low
IRON	(See text, page 63.)			

has received a great deal of attention in the press. In reality, very few babies have this problem. However, if your baby does become colicky, has loose stool after she eats, or refuses to eat, have your doctor check for this and other potential problems. Even when lactose intolerance is diagnosed, milk doesn't have to be completely eliminated. Breast-feeding will not be possible, but lactose in milk or formula can be predigested with a preparation called Lact-Aid, now on the market.

The iron content of most milks is low. However, breast-fed babies don't develop anemia, while those fed diluted cow's milk do. Cow's milk that is not properly heat-treated causes the baby to lose some blood from its stomach and intestines. In addition, only ten percent of the iron in cow's milk is absorbed, while fifty percent or more of the iron in breast milk is absorbed. The absorption of iron from today's infant formulas is nearly as good as from breast milk.

Cow's milk is fortified with vitamin D, and all formulas contain a good supply of this vitamin. The amount in human milk is quite low. Vitamin D, of course, is needed for the absorption of calcium. There is some controversy about whether or not vitamin D supplements should be given to fully breast-fed infants. A number of cases of rickets caused by vitamin D deficiency have been reported in fully breast-fed babies. But most of these children were breast-fed for at least six months, with no other food source of vitamin D. The mothers were following various strict vegetarian (no milk) or fad diets. The condition became severe enough for parents to seek medical care in the winter or early spring. Breast milk contains less vitamin D in the winter than summer due to the difference in time the mother is exposed to sunlight. In these cases, vitamin D supplements should be given to the baby.

As you can see, infant formulas increasingly approach breast milk in terms of nutrient composition. However, there is one difference that will likely always remain: the special immunizing properties of breast milk will probably never be duplicated. Breast milk contains immunoglobulins (very large amounts in early breast milk, especially colostrum), antibacterial factors, white blood cells, and the ability to promote the growth of "friendly" bacteria. All of these help in protecting the baby from illness.

For many years, it was argued that these substances weren't important in our relatively sanitary society. However, more and more studies reveal that breast-fed babies have fewer gastrointestinal, upper respiratory, and inner ear infections. So while breast-feeding may not be critical to the actual survival of your baby, it will partly shield her from these worrisome problems.

Breast-feeding also means that the baby's gastrointestinal tract is not exposed to materials that would produce allergies. Breast-feeding has been especially beneficial in reducing the problem in babies who come from families with a history of allergies.

It has been suggested that breast-feeding may help to prevent infant obesity, sudden infant death, heart disease, and multiple sclerosis. No conclusive proof exists, though, to confirm this.

THE TRUTH ABOUT BREAST-FEEDING

You may be convinced of all the good things about breast-feeding, but still be a little doubtful because of a few old myths. Let's dispel a few of these.

Many women can't nurse their babies. Not true; virtually every woman can breast-feed. The five percent who can't either have a contagious disease, inverted nipples, or babies with cleft palate (the last two conditions are extremely rare).

Breast-feeding will ruin the shape of your breasts. Pregnancy causes the breasts to lose their firmness, not breast-feeding.

Small breasts mean too little milk. The amount of milk produced is not at all related to breast size. The number and extent of breast-feeding periods will control how much milk will be produced.

The baby may be allergic to its mother's milk. There is not one known case of this. However, babies may become allergic or intolerant to something that is transferred in milk. If your baby gets an upset stomach or has any other reaction after being breast-fed, check what foods *you've* had. Strong flavors such as onion or garlic will come through in the milk. Modify your diet rather than switch to formula.

You may enjoy some direct benefits of breast-feeding. The hormones produced during lactation cause muscles of the uterus to contract. This may be a little painful at times but helps your uterus to return to a normal size much faster. The return of menstruation is also delayed by breast-feeding. This will help you keep that extra iron you accumulated in your blood during pregnancy.

If you decide to breast-feed but are afraid of failure, remember that it takes three things to make breast-feeding successful: a newborn baby, a new mother, and—most of all—confidence.

Your baby doesn't have to be taught a thing. It's born with a rooting, sucking reflex. Put it anywhere close to a breast, and if it's hungry it will try to find a meal. This reflex may be delayed if the baby is premature or if the mother is given a lot of sedatives during labor.

A new mother is not actually essential to the operation—just a woman. There are cultures where grand-
mothers breast-feed the babies while the mothers work in
the fields. In more and more reported cases, women have
successfully breast-fed *adopted* babies. The main factor is
confidence. And here, hormones are the key.

Two hormones are necessary for milk production—
prolactin and oxytocin. Prolactin causes the breast tissues
to produce milk and oxytocin causes milk to be released—
the "let-down reflex." The baby's sucking stimulates the
breast, which causes oxytocin to be produced and the milk
to flow. You may notice milk droplets coming out of the
nipple that your baby is not using.

The "let-down reflex" is sensitive to a lack of confidence, to fatigue, to interruptions and distractions. Breast-
feeding needs relaxed, quiet times for you and the baby to
establish what has been called the "nursing couple."

After birth, your baby will likely need to be fed every
three hours, including night feedings. This doesn't mean
that you're not producing enough milk, but that breast
milk is more rapidly digested and absorbed than formula.
After the baby is born, it may lose up to ten percent of its
birth weight; this is normal because it was born with extra
water. The weight will soon be regained with frequent
breast-feedings.

More and more women are seeing nursing as a feminine (and feminist) activity. More mothers are breast-
feeding and more continue to nurse for several months.
This trend began with the more highly educated women,
but now has spread to women in all segments of society.
Doctors and nurses are also becoming aware of the benefits
of breast-feeding. But few are yet fully knowledgeable of

the necessary techniques. Unfortunately, most prenatal and mother-craft classes will discuss formula preparation in detail with little or no information on nursing.

If at all possible, join the La Leche League, or the Childbirth Education Association. These worldwide organizations of nursing mothers offer advice and encouragement to women who want to breast-feed. Contact them as early as possible, because you'll need to make preparations before the baby is born. Proper nipple care and breast massage, for instance, should begin six to eight weeks before childbirth. If there is no group or leader in your community, you can get excellent materials from:

La Leche League
International, Inc.
Canadian Supply Depot
Box 39
Williamsburg, Ontario
K0C 2H0

And in the U.S.:
La Leche League International
9616 Minneapolis Avenue
Franklin Park, Illinois
60131

Eating Strategy   *Nursing Mother*

Look after yourself while you are nursing; this also is a time when your body needs increased energy. Your diet should be essentially the same as during the last part of your pregnancy: two servings of high-protein foods, two to four servings of fruits and vegetables, three to four servings of bread, and emphasis on the milk products (an equivalent of four cups a day). More of these foods can be used if you find you need more energy—we suggest you increase the fruits, vegetables, and whole grain cereals. However, now is the time to lose extra weight you may have had before the pregnancy, or have gained during it.

If you are fully breast-feeding, you'll produce about two and one-third cups (or 600 mL) of milk each day at the start, and over three cups (800 mL) a day by the third month. That's 375 and 500 calories a day.

Continue to eat the good iron foods, in case you decreased your stores slightly during the pregnancy. What you eat can affect the amount and quality of your milk to a degree. But the milk production is not as likely to suffer as you are.

In many parts of the world, women who are severely malnourished produce enough milk for their babies. A lot of the hormone prolactin is produced to enable the body tissues to produce that milk. In well-nourished women, less prolactin is required for adequate milk production. This hormonal difference likely accounts for the fact that breast-feeding is more effective in keeping the malnourished woman from becoming pregnant again.

Milk is eighty-seven percent water, so watch your fluid as well as food intake. If you don't drink enough water and other beverages, you will produce the same amount of milk but you'll also produce very concentrated urine. This may lead to kidney infections, or kidney stones, if you are prone to them.

What about the nutrients in *breast milk*? Are these affected by what you eat? One nutrient that is definitely affected by your diet is fat—not the amount in the milk, but the type. Average breast milk used to contain six percent linoleic acid (polyunsaturated fatty acid). Since we've started using more polyunsaturated oils and margarines in recent years, this has increased to sixteen percent. There is no reason to believe that this does the baby any harm.

Breast milk contains vitamins and minerals. Some of

these are influenced slightly by the amount of vitamins and minerals in your diet. Some women who were given supplements had more vitamin B_6, vitamin B_{12}, and riboflavin in their milk. However, the increases were only slight; well-nourished women who did not use the supplements had adequate amounts of these nutrients in their milk.

Unfortunately, other substances besides nutrients can be transferred to breast milk. The materials you need to be most concerned about are such pesticides as DDT, dieldrin, aldrin and heptachlor, and industrial chemicals, especially polychlorinated biphenyls (PCBs). The widespread use of pesticides has either been banned or severely restricted in many parts of North America. Their concentration in human milk has been progressively declining since 1970.

PCBs are also not used as much as they once were, but they remain in water and accumulate in fresh-water fish. They are still used in some industries. There has been no reported case of poisoning from either pesticides or PCBs, but you should be aware of the possibilities. To keep your risk low while you're pregnant or nursing:

Do not eat fresh-water fish, especially game fish caught in water known to be contaminated with PCBs (for example, the Great Lakes). Use ocean fish instead. Use only lean meat to minimize the amount of DDT and other pesticides you get. These substances accumulate in animal fat.

Don't go on a crash diet. As you lose weight, the potentially dangerous materials will be released into your blood from your fat to be transferred to your baby or milk.

Have your breast milk checked if you work in a factory making transformers or other equipment containing

PCBs, or if you have accidently been exposed to a large amount of pesticides.

FORMULAS

Modern *commercial formulas* are skillfully designed to meet the baby's nutritional needs. Several generations have been started on formula with no obvious detrimental effect. Formulas are nutritionally complete and no supplement should be used. The ideal formula should be as close to breast milk as possible, except if a change in protein or carbohydrate is necessary because of an allergy or intolerance.

The main disadvantage to bottle-feeding is that you have more control over how much your baby eats. (In breast-feeding, only your baby decides.) Be careful to avoid force-feeding. There's no good evidence that bottle-fed babies are fatter than breast-fed babies, but this could happen if you continuously push your baby to finish the last drop in every bottle.

Cow's milk should never be fed directly to young babies because it contains too much protein and minerals. However, an adequate *home formula* may be made by mixing three ounces (100 mL) of evaporated milk, four and one-half ounces (130 mL) of water and two teaspoons (10 mL) of corn syrup. If single feeds are prepared under very clean conditions, bacterial contamination is not a problem. Boiling or overheating cow's milk formula destroys two-thirds of the folic acid; some babies fed these formulas have developed folic acid deficiencies as a result. Keep the opened can of evaporated milk refrigerated.

Babies fed mostly or entirely on cow's milk formula should be given two milligrams of vitamin C and seven milligrams of iron each day. If the milk does not already have vitamin D added, 400 I.U. of this nutrient should be given each day too.

If your water supply contains less than 0.7 ppm. of fluoride, a fluoride supplement should be given as outlined in the following eating strategy.

 Eating Strategy   *Baby*

There's a myth that babies know instinctively what they should eat. Anyone who watches a small baby knows that this isn't true. Everything goes in the mouth—dirt, old cigarette stubs, razor blades, and so on. This is part of the baby's way of exploring its environment.

Some studies show that even babies who are given a wide range of good foods to choose from don't select a variety that will meet their needs. One child turned yellow because she ate only canned peaches, which contain a lot of yellow carotene—a type of vitamin A.

So it's up to you to see that your baby is well fed.

BIRTH TO 4 TO 6 MONTHS

Breast milk supplemented with fluoride, vitamin D, and perhaps iron. (Breast-feed for two weeks at the very least, so your baby will get the unique food—colostrum.)

Theoretically, breast milk is the perfect food for a baby. But some recent evidence indicates that vitamin D and perhaps iron in breast milk may not meet the baby's needs, particularly if the mother does not have a good supply of these nutrients herself. If you are completely breast-feeding your child, you may be wise to give her 400 I.U. of vitamin D and seven milligrams of supplemental iron each day. As your child gets older, these nutrients can come from vitamin D-fortified milk and iron-fortified baby cereals. Do not give more than the recommended amounts of supplements. Babies and young children are *very* sensitive to overdoses of nutrients. See p. 194 for a list of symptoms of nutrient toxicities.

Commercial formula with no supplements

Many formulas come either with or without iron. Some experts suggest that the iron formula should be used from birth. Others believe that it is not necessary until your baby is six months old. If you were getting a good supply of iron, your baby will have a good supply stored in her liver when she is born.

6 TO 12 MONTHS

Breast milk or formula (iron-fortified), still the primary food

Do not use skim or partially skimmed milk during the first twelve months. It is too low in calories and does not contain enough essential fatty acids necessary for growth and for development of the baby's nerves. The low fat intake may lead to lower body fat, which limits the baby's ability to withstand a long illness.

Introduce solid foods in this order:

Introduce one new food a week to check whether the baby may be

1. fortified cereals
starting with rice
2. vegetables
3. fruits
4. meats
5. mixed dishes
Finger foods such as
cottage cheese, toast,
or zwieback can also
be introduced.

allergic or intolerant to it. During
the time when formula, breast
milk, or cow's milk is the major
food, experiment to see what your
child likes. And continue to offer
as large a variety as possible from
among these foods. Also, try some
of the foods she's rejected before.
Tastes change, even for babies.

AFTER 12 MONTHS

whole or partly skimmed milk
variety of soft adult foods

2 WEEKS TO 16 YEARS—FLUORIDE SUPPLEMENTS

Fluoride is an essential nutrient that is very low in breast
milk, cow's milk and even powdered formula prepared
with unfluoridated water. (Premixed formulas should not
be supplemented.) As fluoride is most effective in
hardening your baby's teeth even before they appear, the
American Academy of Pediatrics recommends that
supplements may be necessary at a very early age for all
babies. The amounts needed, of course, will depend on the
fluoride content of your drinking water. If it's more than
0.7 ppm. no supplements are necessary. If it's 0.3 to 0.7
ppm., 0.25 mg of fluoride should be given each day (as
drops or pills) to children from two to three years old; 0.50
mg per day for those three to sixteen. If the fluoride level is
less than 0.3 ppm. these amounts should be increased to
0.25 mg per day from two weeks to two years; 0.50 mg per
day from two to three years; and 1.0 mg per day from three
to sixteen years. Note: Fluoride can be toxic, and in larger
amounts can cause brown spots on teeth and other
undesirable side effects.

After deciding whether to breast-feed or bottle-feed,

the next big question to settle is the time to start using baby foods. Some guidelines preceded. Many people, however, seem to ignore them. Many studies show that infant foods are being used extensively before three months, and some mothers try to introduce them as early as two weeks.

There are several reasons why the early introduction of baby foods is not necessary, and may even be undesirable. First, breast milk, with the supplements recommended, or an iron-fortified formula, supply all the nutrients your baby will need until four to six months of age.

Second, the very young baby is geared for sucking, not for eating solids. To suck, she pushes her tongue up against the top of her mouth. If you give her solid food, it will come out, not go down her throat. She's not spitting it out on purpose, she just doesn't know what to do with it yet.

Another objection to the early introduction of solid foods is that the baby cannot adequately let you know when it doesn't want any more. And there is a great tendency to overfeed—to want the baby to "just finish this last little bite."

Solid food may be introduced more for the parents' benefit than for the baby's. There is a lot of pressure (advertising and otherwise) to start baby foods early. Some mothers believe that feeding solid foods causes the baby to sleep longer—maybe through the night. If this does happen, it is likely due to some overfeeding.

Start introducing solid foods between the first four and six months of the baby's life. If you're breast-feeding, continue the vitamin D and fluoride supplements. If you're using formula, start cutting back the amount to about thirty ounces (900 mL) a day. (You may want to use the formula until nearly the end of the baby's first year.)

However, you could begin to substitute whole milk, or evaporated milk (diluted with an equal amount of water). Don't use skim or partly skimmed milk, because it doesn't supply enough calories. Also, the fat and protein in milk nicely balance the solid foods that are initially high carbohydrate foods.

Use a baby cereal first—perhaps rice cereals, which are usually well tolerated. Cereals are fortified with iron—ferrous sulphate, which is very readily absorbed. (Fortified cereals not prepared especially for babies contain iron that is not so well absorbed). This iron can replace the iron supplement used with either breast milk or cow's milk. Other cereals can be introduced, one or two a week to make sure your baby is not allergic to them.

Then introduce vegetables. Some people find that vegetables are not as well accepted if they are introduced after fruits. Next the fruits and finally meats. There is no reason to use the prepared exotic mixed foods. You can get more protein by mixing a bit of meat and vegetable foods at home. And sweetened desserts can be eliminated entirely. Recently, it has been shown that some baby foods, particularly fruits and vegetables, decrease the absorption of iron from breast milk. On the other hand, other foods such as meat and those containing vitamin C increase the absorption. While eggs and spinach contain a lot of iron, it is not well absorbed.

Because of the effect of fruits and vegetables on the absorption of iron from breast milk, don't give them to your baby at the same time that you're nursing. Instead, give your baby one milk-free meal a day of cereal, meat, and vitamin C food, including the fruits and vegetables.

Eggs have often been emphasized in infants' diets. They contain high-quality protein. However, some babies are sensitive to the protein in the yolk. They may have to eat only the whites, or avoid eggs entirely.

COMMERCIAL BABY FOODS

There are a great variety of these available. They are safe, convenient, nutritionally good, and a bit expensive. Most are made without sugar and salt. Some still contain modified starches, which add calories but dilute the vitamins, minerals, and protein. As with other foods—be a label reader.

You may taste your baby's food and find it is almost tasteless. Resist the temptation to flavor it with sugar or salt. Babies have many more tastebuds than adults, and to them, this food is just great.

A note of caution—don't heat baby foods in the jars they come in in a microwave oven. Pressure builds up, causing the food to explode through the small mouth of the jar. You can heat these foods in wide-mouth containers or bowls.

HOME-MADE BABY FOODS

Completely nutritious foods can be made at home. We recommend you use infant cereals for the available iron, but all other types of food can be made from what the rest of the family is having. Strained regular unsweetened fruit juices are as good as the juices packaged for babies. Don't feed them to the baby by bottle as a pacifier. Natural sugars will cause cavities in the little teeth even faster than milk.

Solid foods will have to be mashed and softened. This can be done either with a fork, a standard blender, or one of the special baby food blenders on the market. The special blender is probably best because you can prepare small amounts—and it's easy to clean. If you decide to buy one, run some bread through to remove any tiny metal shavings that may still be on the blades.

Start with some foods that are pretty soft to begin with—cooked apples or pumpkin, bananas, baked potato, cottage cheese. A recent study found that a popular new baby food was yoghurt. As with commercial baby foods, it's best to start with single item foods and introduce one or two a week to check for possible allergic reactions.

If possible, use fresh or frozen fruits and vegetables. They are less likely to contain added salt and sugar (and won't be contaminated by lead) than canned foods. (Don't worry, cans designed for baby foods are made so that lead contamination is not a problem.) Don't overcook the foods, and don't add salt or sugar.

Take precautions when you prepare the baby's food; make sure that everything—foods, pans, hands—is clean. And only make as much as the baby will eat in one sitting, or store the extra in the refrigerator no more than twenty-four hours. If you want to make larger batches, freeze portions, perhaps in plastic ice cube trays. Thaw and heat just the amount you need for each meal.

WEANING

There's no one perfect time to replace breast-feeding or the bottle with a cup. This will depend on your child's ability to handle the cup and her inclination to use it.

By twelve months of age, neither breast milk nor formula are necessary, so the change to whole or partially skimmed milk may be the time to start weaning.

TEETHING FOODS

It's a great event when the first little tooth appears, around ten months. The full set of baby teeth will be out at about twenty-four months.

Your baby's new ability to chew means that she's ready to take on a few crunchy foods such as dry toast or zwieback. She'll enjoy the variety and it's great exercise for her jaws at the same time. Gradually move to small pieces of sliced liver, chicken, or other meat, soft chunks of vegetables and fruits.

And protect those little teeth. They're very sensitive to decay. Too many babies suffer from the nursing bottle syndrome—cavities on the insides of the front teeth. This is caused, as we mentioned, by propping a baby up with a bottle—either milk, fruit juice, or (heaven forbid) sugar water—and letting her suck off and on for a long time. This is especially harmful if used as a way to get her to go to sleep.

Let her finish all she wants, then rinse her mouth out with water and wipe her teeth with a damp soft cloth. It would be a good idea to do this at every feeding. As she gets older, get a soft baby toothbrush and start brushing her teeth. You may not be very successful at first, but she'll learn that teeth need to be cleaned. A trip to a pedontist (a dentist specializing in children) around age two and one-half to three may be a good idea to check alignment of baby teeth before the second set comes in.

BABIES AND BOTULISM—A SPECIAL NOTE

Honey should not be given to babies less than twelve months old. The first reason for this recommendation is that babies do not really need honey. The second, more important reason is that there have been some cases of infant botulism traced to the use of honey.

The spores of clostriduim botulism may contaminate raw honey; these are not destroyed by current processing methods. For some reason, these spores germinate in the intestines of babies (but not adults) and produce a deadly neurotoxin.

Although infant botulism is a relatively rare disease, some physicians believe it is a potential cause of perhaps five percent of the deaths from Sudden Infant Death syndrome. The neurotoxin acts either by directly paralyzing the diaphragm or by obstructing the upper airways.

In the classical food-borne botulism, the bacteria spores themselves do not cause the problems. However, they can produce a potent neurotoxin in foods, particularly improperly canned foods. It is this neurotoxin that causes the symptoms in older children and adults.

SPECIAL BABIES

A fat baby is a healthy baby. Or is it? While no one believes that this is always the case, you must be a little wary of believing the opposite. A fat baby is not necessarily an unhealthy baby.

Newborn babies are about sixteen percent fat. These fat stores serve as an energy reserve that can be used if your baby becomes sick and can't eat for a while.

The number of fat cells increases during infancy, early childhood, and adolescence. There is a possibility that overeating during these times causes more fat cells to develop—fat cells that will be with the person for the rest of life. Not all fat babies, however, become fat children, then fat adults. If you have a plump child, don't panic, but keep an eye on her. As she starts to grow she will likely thin out. If not, you have time to slightly restrict her food intake in line with your doctor's recommendations. Don't put her on a diet, just slow down her weight gain until she grows taller.

Bottle-feeding and the early introduction of solid

foods have at times been blamed for fat babies. However, this doesn't always seem to be the case. (Of course, we encourage breast-feeding and later introduction of solid foods for other reasons discussed earlier in this chapter.)

Not only are there now more preterm and *low birth weight* babies being born, more of them, even the tiniest, are surviving. Therefore, it has been important to look for the best way to feed them.

These tiny babies grow even more rapidly than full-term infants. Normal breast milk and formulas do not contain enough protein, phosophorus, calcium, and vitamin D. Cow's milk contains too much total minerals. Special formulas are being tested. These have more proteins (most as the easily digested whey proteins), calcium, phosophorus, and vitamin D. They also contain a type of fat, called medium chain triglycerides, which is easily digested.

But another food seems likely to be the proper one for these babies—their own mother's milk. Why would you expect this to be any different from any other human milk? Because of the kangaroo.

The newborn kangaroo is a tiny, immature creature which crawls into its mother's pouch, attaches itself to a teat, and stays there drinking milk until it is fully mature. The pouch may also be occupied by an older brother or sister (a "joey"), who makes use of the other teat. Each teat produces an entirely different milk. Similarly, human mothers of premature babies produce milk appropriate to these children rather than to the full-term infant.

Recent studies have analyzed the milk of women shortly after they have given birth to premature babies. Their milk was found to have what the tiny child needs— more protein and other nitrogen compounds, less lactose and more calcium, sodium, and chloride than milk of women with full-term infants. While a tiny newborn infant can't nurse well enough to be breast-fed, some mothers are experimenting with collecting their milk and feeding it to the baby. Manual breast pumps are available from many medical supply stores.

4 The Care and Feeding of Children

Children, whether you have one or a dozen, are both a trial and a joy. It's a joy to watch them grow and learn. But it's also sometimes difficult to cope with their individual problems.

If you have two or more children you know the problem! Even if you have only one, he or she is probably not at all like the model child you read about. Each child is an individual—and that applies to eating habits as well as other aspects of life. Early childhood years are when eating habits are established. What you give your child will partly influence this, but her own preferences will have an impact too.

Eating Strategy *Children*

The following would be a good guide for children from two to twelve years. Increase the number and size of servings according to the child's own growth pattern and appetite.

FOOD	AMOUNT/DAY	NUTRIENTS
Water	3-6 glasses	(water is an essential nutrient too)
Milk, fortified	2-4 glasses	calcium, riboflavin, protein, vitamins A and D
Margarine	4 tsp. (20 mL)	essential fatty acids
Meat group	1 to 2 servings	protein, minerals, B vitamins
Whole wheat or enriched breads and cereals	4 or more servings	protein, minerals, B vitamins, fiber
Vegetables	2 servings, other than potatoes (1 dark green, leafy, or deep yellow)	vitamins A and C, fiber
Fruits	2 servings (1 citrus)	
Eggs	3 per week	protein, iron, other minerals and vitamins

Your child can start selecting foods from each group when she's very young. Remember that habits, good or bad, usually remain when they are started early. Each stage of your child's growth can often mean new challenges for you, as different nutritional needs occasionally clash with her distinct—and vocal!—preferences.

TODDLERS

After one year, your child's growth slows. Her legs grow longer and she has less fat. Even the plump baby will generally grow taller while gaining very little weight.

Interestingly enough, the actual *total* amount of food and calories she needs now may be actually less than she needed a few months before. Her eating may be erratic. As she discovers the powerful word "no," she may become very assertive, reject foods (even yesterday's favorites), refuse to eat, or refuse to feed herself. Sound familiar?

This can be a very trying period for parents. Try to be patient and tolerant. A hungry child will eat, especially if she's given a chance to learn what hunger really is. Don't be over-anxious, and don't bribe with food. Let her learn to respond to her own hunger signals. Too many adults can trace their weight problems to the "lovin'" food their mothers forced them to eat, and the "clean-your-plate" syndrome.

A young child still needs growth nutrients—protein, calcium, phosphorus, and vitamin D. That's why milk (as a beverage, or in cheese and other foods) still plays such an important role in her diet. Two to three cups a day, however, will be adequate. Much more than that may replace other needed foods. If she's a real "milk-aholic," save the milk until after or between meals.

If you need to cut down the calories or are concerned about fat intake, start using 2% or skim milk now, or, for an acceptable and inexpensive intermediate, make 1% milk by mixing equal parts of 2% fat milk and reconstituted skim milk powder.

By the time your child is one year old she'll have two to six teeth. With these she's ready to tackle a large variety of foods, softer, smaller pieces of table foods and crunchy, crisp foods. But she may not want to. Perhaps you'll be lucky and have one who'll eat anything set before her! But usually kids reject a lot—especially vegetables.

Ingenious ways have been tried to get kids to eat vegetables—changing how they're cut or cooked, or even using reverse psychology and forbidding them because they're grown-up foods. This may help some, but the better way is probably to consider the child's whole eating environment and include the types of foods she *will* eat.

Children like simple foods—foods they can identify. No sauces or casseroles. Foods shouldn't be highly seasoned (seasoning is really not necessary at all). And serve them at moderate temperatures (even lukewarm milk). Finger foods are more readily accepted because the child can handle these herself. Try raw vegetable sticks as a substitute for cooked vegetables.

Meal times should be pleasant times for both you and your child. Allow a quiet time before the meal so she's relaxed and not too excited. Provide dishes and spoons of the right size so she can start learning to feed herself. And be prepared for the mess—fortunately children are washable. Just make sure the place they eat in is washable too.

Food is not a reward for good behavior or punishment for bad. It's not a substitute for time and attention or a pacifier to calm an angry, tired, or bored child. The messages you give your child about food are as important as the nutrients in it. Future eating habits will be largely determined by what your child thinks food is and how it should be used.

The nutrients that a child needs are no different from those an adult needs. The difference lies in the *amount*. The total amount needed is, of course, smaller, but it is larger in relation to the child's size. For example, a young child needs 1.5 to 2.0 grams of protein per kilogram of body weight. An adult needs only 0.7 to 1.0 grams per kilogram.

One-half to two-thirds of this protein should be high-quality protein (animal protein and soybean protein). A child can get all the high-quality protein she needs from milk or eggs. We do not recommend that you try to raise your child on a pure vegetarian diet—that is, no animal products at all—unless you get a great deal of information about the proper way to mix vegetable proteins. Even with that she may not get enough calcium and may not grow normally.

Other nutrients that are of prime importance for the growing child are iron, vitamin C, and vitamin A. These are the vitamins that are low in many children's diets. Check the eating strategy for good sources.

PRESCHOOLERS (THREE TO SIX YEARS)

Much of what we've said about the younger child still holds true in this age group. By three years of age, your child should be eating a good variety of foods—or at least be familiar with them. The eating strategy for children serves as a good guide for all of childhood. Only the number and size of servings and the variety of foods need to increase.

Even at this age, your child needs snacks for extra energy and nutrition. These should be considered as part of the total food intake and not include sticky, sugary foods that will promote tooth decay. By about two years of age, your child has her full set of baby teeth, and she needs to keep them healthy until they're replaced by her permanent teeth. (If you want to use a little bribery here, tell her that the Tooth Fairy pays more for teeth with no holes in them.)

What does begin to change as your child enters this age period are the variety of influences on her eating pattern. Television, nursery school, and larger groups of friends promote ideas about food that may or may not correspond with what you have been trying to teach.

The big "educator" (or brain-washer) is television. A young child is particularly vulnerable to television's influence. There are many excellent programs (*Sesame Street, Mr. Rogers, Polka Dot Door*) that stimulate the preschooler's imagination and are highly educational. But television also includes commercials—lots of them. One study showed that children's prime time (Saturday morning) devoted more time to advertising than any other time in the week. And over ninety percent of these commercials were for some type of food product.

In general, the poorer the nutritional quality of a food, the more money will be spent on advertising it. Many commercials are designed to give your child the idea that all foods have to be sweet or chocolaty, strawberry or otherwise flavored, or that you should drink *anything* but water. Breakfast cereals too, especially the highly sugared, are advertised as fun and exciting. (There are some exceptions: good commercials for fruit, juice, and whole grain products. One commercial even sells the *idea* of eating breakfast.)

So while you're watching over the TV programs your kids watch, think of the commercials as well. You may have to make a special effort to counteract the powerful messages a young child gets from most food advertising.

Another important consideration at this period affects many mothers. More and more young children are being cared for outside their own homes—by babysitters, nursery schools, or daycare centers. Good daycare is sometimes difficult to find; while you're investigating all of the details of the type of daycare you choose, be sure to look at the food.

Many daycare centers are registered by the government. There are nutritional guidelines for these centers, and, fortunately, many daycare teachers are required to take courses in nutrition. But the daycare offered by your neighbor, or the woman on the next block, doesn't have to meet such standards, so make sure you know how your child will be fed.

A child may spend up to nine hours away from home. She should get food appropriate for that time—lunch, two or three snacks, maybe even breakfast. If breakfast is not included, the food supplied to your child should contain one-third to one-half of her requirements for the day.

As vital as the basic nutrients are, that's not the only thing to check with your daycare center or sitter. Attitudes are equally important. At this age, your child still has a lot to learn about food. What are the attitudes of the teacher or sitter towards nutrition? Do they consider it important? What are they trying to teach the child? Be sure to ask.

Some years ago the Head Start Program in the United States developed an excellent system of both feeding children and teaching them about food. The children learned to grow food or see how it was grown, and to prepare and serve it. They learned the whole meaning of food: its color, texture, taste, relation to other foods and to health. These are essential experiences for a child.

When you're caring for your child at home, you too

are teaching — continually. Your attitudes will be picked up quickly. Do you take your child shopping, let her help select her food and suggest family meals? (Limits apply, of course; a jellybean lunch is going too far!) Is your kitchen off-limits when you're cooking, or can little hands "help" even if it means more work for you?

It's not too early for them to start helping with the food preparation, scrubbing vegetables, flipping pancakes, or decorating milk puddings with fruit slices. The pay-off for you is that they will almost always eat what they prepare — no matter what it tastes or looks like.

At the start, create a "kitchen-conscious" child. As early as possible, help her develop a working knowledge of the importance of safety in the kitchen. Stress the importance of keeping knives sharp, handles of pots and pans turned away from the front of the stove, electrical cords and plugs in good condition, floors free of slippery spills, all equipment clean and in proper working order.

Here are two tried-and-true favorites with preschoolers that will help convince your child that all good snacks may not be advertised on TV!

YOGHURT POPSICLES
2 cups (500 mL) plain yoghurt
1 cup (250 mL) fruit (strawberries, bananas,
   etc.)
5 ice cream cones, flat bottomed
Blend yoghurt and fruit in blender. Pour into ice cream cones and freeze.

ANTS-ON-A-LOG
celery
peanut butter or cheese spread
raisins

Wash and clean celery stalks. Cut into pieces. Fill each piece with peanut butter or cheese spread. Put raisins (ants) on top of peanut butter.

SCHOOL AGE (SIX TO TWELVE YEARS)

Nutritional needs and the nutritional problems during this stage continue to be the same. Growth nutrients, proteins, calcium, vitamins A and C, should still be emphasized, but in larger amounts.

But distraction is a new problem! School, friends, and after-school activities all compete for your child's attention and meal times can be lost in the shuffle. For meals that your children eat at home, the word is involvement. Sit down with them and plan the week's meals together. Have them help make out the grocery list.

By this age they can even begin some serious cooking. The best meal to start with is breakfast—the one most likely skipped and the one most essential to school performance. Breakfast should supply about one-third of your child's total daily requirements and should include foods from at least three of the four food groups—milk and milk products, meat and alternatives, breads and cereals, fruit and vegetables.

Kids might be more interested in breakfast if they realize it doesn't have to feature the usual bacon and fried egg. Breakfast can be last night's leftover pizza or even a cold chicken leg and hunk of cheese! Break the rules for traditional breakfast fare, but don't shortchange nutritional needs. Have them try these "short orders" for themselves. Of course, you'll need to round some of them out in full-fledged breakfasts.

- a slice of raisin bread with cheddar cheese (try this grilled)
- graham crackers spread with peanut butter
- a bowl of yoghurt topped with sliced fruit
- hot rolls or muffins with dried apricots and cheese
- hard-cooked eggs or egg salad on slice of whole wheat bread
- ice-cream or frozen yoghurt balls topped with crushed cereal
- french toast with unsweetened applesauce and nutmeg
- canned peaches or fruit cocktail (preferably packed without sugar) on hot oatmeal or cold cereal
- a glass of eggnog, milkshake, or hot chocolate

If your child takes her lunch to school, help her start to prepare this. The more stirring, mixing, and assembling she does, the less likely that the lunch will be traded for a friend's chocolate bar or tossed in the garbage.

Variety is the spice of life—and especially for bag lunches. Without a little planning they can get pretty dreary. Vary the type of bread bought for sandwiches. Crusty rolls, hamburger and hot dog buns, rye, whole wheat, and oatmeal breads are ways of making sandwiches less monotonous. Grated carrots, shredded cabbage, bean sprouts, olives, pickles, all dress up any standard sandwich fillings. And crisp raw vegetables add "crunch to lunch."

If your child has meals at a school with a cafeteria or catering service, check into the foods offered (including the vending machines!). You may be lucky enough to find one where a qualified dietitian and a student committee plan a variety of meals. On the other hand, some "get-rich-quick" schemes may cater to the persistent demand for foods that are high in energy (calories), salt, and fat and low in other nutrients. One school, for example, offered such products — "fortified" to increase the nutrient value. But that did nothing to solve the fat, calorie, and salt problems. Nor did it help the students learn about how to eat in the real world, where these products are *not* over-fortified. There are some excellent catering companies, however, that not only supply nutritious meals and snacks but supply ingenious and reliable nutrition education as well.

Double-check the amount of spending money your children have. Is most of it going for in-between snacks at the local fast food outlet? A good home supply of such school munchies as cheese cubes, raisins, plain yoghurt with fruit, celery stuffed with peanut butter, bags of peanuts, or fresh fruit might discourage this habit.

If you're working away from home (or even if you're not) you'll do your children and yourself a service by helping them learn to cook. Some families start by having each young member of the family plan, shop for, and prepare one special meal a month, then one a week, then for a whole week each month. Buy your child her own cookbook and present it as a most precious gift.

Give your children these recipes as a start. They've been child-tested and given the nod of approval.

SUPER SANDWICHES

Here's a recipe that's a favorite for people of all ages. It's quick, colorful, easy, and quite inexpensive. Pita bread, fresh or frozen, is sold in most supermarkets.

1 head of lettuce, torn in bite-size pieces

1 small tin tuna fish or flaked ham
1 cup (250 mL) cheese cubes

Add a handful of a mixture of the following:
spinach
red cabbage, shredded
carrots, shredded or thinly sliced
Bermuda onion, sliced
bean sprouts
mushrooms, sliced
radishes, sliced
celery, sliced
cucumbers, sliced
watercress
green peppers, sliced or diced
kidney beans or chick peas (cooked)

oil and vinegar dressing
pita bread

Prepare bread by cutting each "round" in half. Gently separate until a pocket forms. Place other ingredients in a large salad bowl. Add oil and vinegar dressing. Toss well. Serve in pita bread pockets. (Allow a half or more "rounds" of pita per serving.)

"SHOOK-UP" SHAKE

Combine 1 cup (250 mL) skim or 2% milk and some bananas, frozen strawberries, or other fruit in the blender, then pour into tall glasses. Using frozen fruit eliminates the need to add ice cream to this drink, and cuts down on fat and sugar.

CORN CHIP CHILI   Serves 5

Children can start this supper dish before parents arrive home from the office. Serve with a green salad, an apple crisp, or fresh fruit.

1 lb. (450 g) lean ground beef
1 tbsp. (15 mL) salad oil
1 cup (250 mL) chopped onions
1 cup (250 mL) chopped green peppers
2 tsp. (10 mL) chili powder
dash of pepper
2½ cups (625 mL) tomatoes
1½ cups (375 mL) corn chips

Brown beef in oil in frying pan. Add onions and green peppers and brown lightly. Add seasonings, tomatoes, and 1 cup (250 mL) corn chips. Cook gently for 35 minutes, stirring occasionally to break up tomatoes. Just before serving, garnish with ½ cup (125 mL) corn chips.

VITAMIN AND MINERAL SUPPLEMENTS

You've seen the ads, "If your child doesn't eat right, just give him a Handy-Dandy Vitamin Pill every day and all will be well." This type of advertising is promoting a potential health hazard: vitamin and mineral overdoses. Overdoses are becoming more common, not because of any problems with the food we eat, but because of our misuse of the highly advertised supplements.

You may have noticed in the eating strategy we outlined that we didn't mention supplements. We don't think they're necessary for most children, even those with rather erratic eating habits. Only a child with some major problem affecting eating or absorption of nutrients needs supplements, and these should be prescribed by a doctor after a thorough review of your child's needs. Despite this, supplements, including those marketed for children, are big business. Interestingly, many surveys have shown that the supplements being used are not the ones that are needed. For example, older girls may need extra iron and calcium, but they're likely taking vitamins C and B's.

A basic one-a-day supplement is generally a waste of money but not a danger. The danger arises with mega or high potency vitamins. These definitely should not be given to children, unless prescribed for a diagnosed condition. Even if they do not cause real illness, some of them may stunt your child's growth.

The other danger is that children, especially the younger ones, will help themselves to a handful of the pills. This has happened — with near fatal results. The symptoms of the most toxic nutrients (see the table) are not specific, that is, they can be the result of other causes. But if you have supplements in the house, for yourself or your child, you should get emergency help if any of these symptoms appear. Check the supplement bottle, and if many are missing take the bottle along to the hospital.

SYMPTOMS OF NUTRIENT OVERDOSE

Vitamin A   Sore and weak bones, dry, cracked skin, vomiting, brittle nails, hair loss, irritability, excessive tiredness, headaches, blurred vision.

Vitamin D   Headaches, weakness, nausea and vomiting, constipation, excessive urination, excessive thirst.

Iron   Lethargy, vomiting, diarrhea, weak pulse, slow heart rate, shock. Two grams of ferrous sulfate (which equal 400 mg of iron) are considered a potentially fatal dose for a young child.

DENTAL CARE

Dental caries (cavities) are the plague of the civilized world. A Nutrition Canada survey found that ninety-six percent of all adults had tooth decay. Forty of every 100 people nineteen years of age or older had their upper or lower (or both) sets of teeth missing.

Dental cavities are so common that we take them for granted. Everyone has them, don't they? The answer is no. Many other societies that suffer types of malnutrition now unknown to us don't have our teeth problems.

You want to protect your children's teeth as long as you can. To do that, it helps to have some idea of how teeth are formed and how they can be damaged. Teeth, and especially the outer layer of enamel, are the hardest tissues of the body. They are essentially a complex mixture of mineral compounds, mostly calcium and phosphate, layered on a protein structure. As children's teeth are growing the minerals are just being deposited, and cavities are most likely to occur. It takes three things to make a cavity — basic susceptibility, bacteria, and food for the bacteria.

Like everything else, different people have different teeth. Some teeth are a beautiful chalky white; unfortunately, these are most easily decayed. Darker teeth are harder because they contain a larger amount of harder calcium phosphate salts.

We can't really change our genetic make-up, but teeth can be hardened by fluoride, which converts the harder calcium salts to even harder calcium fluoride salts. The best way to get fluoride is in water or food. Fluoride then goes through the blood; all of the tooth minerals are affected. While fluoride treatments or fluoride toothpastes are good, only the outside enamel layer benefits.

Unfortunately, few foods contain much fluoride, and

most water contains even less, so many water systems have added fluoride at about one part per million. This amount is sufficient to help make hard teeth but not cause any adverse effects. (Fluoride in larger amounts can turn teeth brown and make bones grow abnormally.)

Some teeth are smooth; others are rough, with crevices where bacteria and food can easily accumulate. There's little to be done, aside from trying to keep the bacteria and food washed out. We can do this only partly, because we have bacteria in our mouths all the time. They attach themselves to the teeth, usually between them or close to the gums, and build up a hard covering, plaque, which makes them very difficult to remove. (Good brushing, flossing, and regular professional cleaning can help.)

The bacteria metabolize the food you supply them, producing acid which dissolves the mineral in the tooth. This exposes the protein, which is then destroyed by the bacteria. And voilà! a cavity. After you eat, the mouth becomes more acidic (due to bacterial activity), and minerals are lost from the teeth. But this acid disappears and minerals from the saliva are replaced in the teeth. This happens regularly, if you don't eat too often. Too much between-meal snacking—particularly with the wrong types of food— keeps the mouth acidic, leaving no time for minerals to be restored.

But snacking is important for children, so rather than trying to eliminate it entirely (probably impossible anyway), it's better to check the types of snacks used. Mouth bacteria prefer carbohydrates, especially sugars, and especially in a nice sticky form that stays on your teeth. It's not the amount of sugar eaten but the length of time it stays in the mouth that's important. (The person who invented all-day suckers must have hated children.)

Eating Strategy *Teeth*

If your water does not contain fluoride, either naturally or added, give your child fluoride drops (0.5 to 1.0 mg per day) until she's sixteen years old (see p. 73).

Sweets eaten at meals are not as damaging as those eaten between meals. For snacks, use foods with protein — milk, cheese, peanut butter — and foods with fiber for cleaning teeth — apples, carrots, et cetera.

Teach good dental care. If your child can't brush after every meal or snack, encourage her to rinse her mouth several times with water to remove as many food particles as possible.

OVERWEIGHT CHILDREN

There are fewer obese children than obese adults, but more and more attention is being paid to the children. Why? Because it is generally believed that it is easier to prevent and treat obesity at this stage rather than later in life.

There is no one simple cause of obesity at any stage of life. Heredity and environment interact to produce a positive calorie balance, which in children is necessary for growth, but carried too far this leads to overweight and true obesity. This means that more energy is being consumed than is being used up, which in chidren, of course, is necessary for growth. But if the intake is too much in excess of requirements, this leads to the overweight.

Numerous factors have been blamed for obese children:

- overweight parents (if both parents are overweight, the child has an eighty percent chance of being overweight too; if only one parent is obese, the chances drop to forty percent)

- large birth weight and rapid early weight gain
- overeating (obese boys were found to eat more and faster than their thinner brothers and classmates)
- inactivity (one study reported that this is the main problem of obese girls)

A recent long-term study of Swedish children found that children who didn't have any of these characteristics were not overweight when they were ten years old and were not overweight when they were sixteen. But interestingly, only fifty percent of the children who had *all* of these characteristics were obese at ten years of age. And not all of the groups studied had been obese when they were younger. So we really don't have the answer to why children are obese yet.

While the amount of fat that children have does change, you need to be concerned about watching this progress and keeping weight under control. According to the U.S. Health Examination Surveys, most fat children become fat teenagers. So whatever the cause of childhood obesity, habits become firmly established at a rather young age and are difficult to change later on.

Eating Strategy   *The Overweight Child*

The treatment will depend on the age of the child, the degree of obesity, and how long it has existed. The first step is a thorough medical examination. If your child is severely overweight, she will require professional help—from a knowledgeable doctor or dietitian or a reputable group that has sessions for children or teens.

The usual approach is to slow weight gain until your child grows to the height that should match her weight. If actual weight loss is necessary, it should be slow, to avoid interference with growth: that means a good, balanced diet with some restriction of high-calorie, low-nutrient foods. (The program outlined in Chapter 7 is applicable here too.)

Changing your child's eating and exercise habits may mean that you'll have to change your own and those of the rest of the family. Ask yourself,

- How many sports or activities do you engage in? Can you increase these and involve your child?
- Does your cooking emphasize low-calorie, low-fat foods, or are scrumptious, calorie-laden desserts your forté?
- Does your child accompany you when you shop, help with menu planning and cooking? Do you discuss basic nutrition?

At all costs, avoid pressuring a child with a weight problem. The resulting emotional stress does far more harm than good. Be sure to emphasize that parental affection and pride are not related to her weight.

THE HYPERACTIVE CHILD

Perhaps nothing has received as much publicity lately as the proposed relationship between certain substances in food and hyperactivity. This theory has been widely proclaimed by Dr. Ben Feingold in *Why Your Child Is Hyper-*

active. He has suggested that children who react to aspirin are also sensitive to similar products called salicylates, which are naturally present in many fruits and vegetables, and to a particular food dye (tartrazine, or Yellow Dye No. 5). He goes on to advise eliminating all foods containing synthesized colors, flavors, and preservatives.

The Feingold diet has become very popular. Feingold groups have sprung up all over North America. The theory, however, has not been as well received by the medical or scientific community, for a number of reasons.

First, there is a major problem in defining hyperactivity. A child can be behaving hyperactively because she's hungry, bored, tired, or simply because she's an energetic, curious child with an exhausted or frustrated parent. Children naturally have what seems to be excess energy and they don't always have the time and space to run it off.

Get a diagnosis from a specialist before you label your child hyperactive. The true hyperactive child is excessively active and restless for her age, has difficulty in concentrating for any length of time, cannot tolerate any frustration, and reacts to it violently. She cannot play by herself and has an unusual lack of fear, to the point of being reckless.

The recommendations of the Feingold diet are based on informal observations rather than on controlled studies. If the diet does work, it's hard to know what part of the diet is responsible. For example, the diet is also low in vitamin C and carbohydrates. Also, children often respond to the extra care and attention they receive when any type of treatment is given.

Careful studies have been done and will continue to be done on this problem. It seems that there are a small number of truly hyperactive children who benefit slightly from the diet, but the results are not nearly as dramatic as promised. Parents may swear by this diet because they are trying to find something, anything, that will work. And the diet may also appear to work because children tend to outgrow the problem as they become teenagers.

Again, we recommend counseling by a specialist. Follow the doctor's advice about medication, about making changes in the child's environment—school and home—and about your own approach to your child.

SPECIAL NUTRITION PROBLEMS

Perhaps because of the great emphasis put on feeding children well in recent years, this age group turns out to be one of the best fed in North America. Anemia, due to too much milk and too little other food, was once a problem, but seems to have been overcome by the introduction of iron-fortified cereals.

Diseases like scurvy (vitamin C deficiency) and beriberi (thiamin deficiency) have generally disappeared from North America. A small number of children of the poorer families show some mild symptoms of these and other deficiencies.

We should not be complacent, however. Children can become malnourished if the proper food and the knowledge of how to use it are not present. In the 1970s, children were again developing rickets (vitamin D deficiency) in the United States. For example, from 1974 to 1978, twenty-four cases were diagnosed in Philadelphia. These were attributed to air pollution and to overdressing the children so that they didn't get much sunlight on their skin. (Vitamin D is produced in our skin when sunlight strikes it.)

In addition, the total intake of vitamin D of these children was very low. Some of the children were being nursed by mothers who were themselves vitamin D-deficient. Others were not given any milk or other foods containing vitamin D because of religious beliefs.

The children most likely to develop rickets and other severe deficiency diseases are those fed pure vegetarian diets, and the only reported cases of protein-calorie malnutrition in North America have been in such children.

As we describe in Chapter 7, a carefully planned vegetarian diet may be fine for an adult. It is not fine for a growing child. A child should be given milk at the very least; the complete protein, calcium, and vitamin D are essential for her growth. The only acceptable substitute is vitamin D-fortified soy milk, but this is not available everywhere.

THE BEST START

What your child eats when she is young will influence her health for the rest of her life. The types of physiological changes we are primarily concerned with today are those that may lead to cardiovascular (heart) disease. Numerous studies have shown that very young children, even babies, in wealthy countries such as the United States and Canada, have streaks of fat in their blood vessels. In some children these streaks disappear, but in others they develop through childhood and adolescence, and then may become real problems as atherosclerosis and heart attacks in adults.

No one knows exactly what causes heart disease, but high amounts of fats (cholesterol and triglycerides) in the blood are considered risk factors. If anyone in your immediate family has heart disease, high blood pressure, or high blood fats, you should have your child checked too. Experts suggest that children with blood triglycerides of more than 140 mg/dL and cholesterol of more than 180 mg/dL should be given medical and dietary advice to control these fats.

If there is no history of these conditions in your family but you want to help your child avoid any problems, first follow some basic advice about eating that you may already use for yourself.

- Cut back on total fats, particularly the saturated (hard) ones.
- Cut out some excess sugars and calories.
- Give your child a good supply of fruits, vegetables, and whole grain breads and cereals.
- Keep salt intake under control. This can be done by using little, if any, salt in your cooking, removing the salt shakers from the table, and making sure salted snacks are eaten only occasionally.

Such diets may delay or prevent many of the health problems that now plague a large part of the adult population.

5 Shortcuts to Family Nutrition

Joan is one of the forty-eight percent of women today who work—at home. She's the mother of a preteen and an active teenager, both of whom are involved in such after-school activities as hockey or soccer, piano and ballet lessons—all of which require juggling meal times and family times together.

"It's hectic enough in winter," says Joan. "My youngest is the goalie, and often hockey practice takes place at the ungodly hour of 6:00 a.m. This means he must get a nourishing breakfast before he goes out—and then something when he gets back, since he's always starving! My daughter's ballet class is right after school, and she's often not home until 6:00 p.m. These activities, combined with the usual jaunts to the dentist and doctor, play havoc with my meal schedule. Yet I want to make sure they're well fed.

"I'm concerned about my husband Jim's eating schedule as well. He's forty, and many colleagues his age have developed hypertension. One of his co-workers has just had a heart attack at forty-eight. As a marketing manager with a computer firm, he's under a lot of stress because the competition is incredible.

"He enjoys sports but feels he has less time for them. He often has an early morning meeting followed by one at 4:00 or 4:30 p.m. He's seldom home before 6:00 or 6:30 p.m., and he's usually exhausted. Several times lately, I've had to wake him when dinner is ready—or he falls asleep in front of the TV.

"When time permits, we like to entertain, and I try to have a dinner party about once every six weeks or so. To add to the confusion, I've just been nominated vice-president of the hospital auxiliary, and that will take me away from home more. I have a demanding schedule, but I like it. Yet I often wonder how I can concentrate on doing the right things. Feeding my family and myself well (and economically) is of prime importance to me. But I'm finding this increasingly difficult to do as the kids and my husband and I get busier."

Joan is like many active North American women: she has a busy family, a career-minded husband, and her own outside interests. There are days when cooking and preparing meals, rushing her family out to various activities on time, running a home and entertaining are simply too much.

If you work outside the home, you will also recognize the problem. Discipline helps. So does delegating — assigning various tasks to various family members. Establishing priorities is important too. Few of us really know where our time goes. Try keeping a time logbook. Many busy people do a lot of things that aren't really necessary. And grocery shopping or meal preparation are activities that others can do, should do, and can be trained to do. But no matter how well disciplined you are, you'll find some time is going to be spent doing things that aren't covered in any schedule you work out: friends phone for help or favors; neighbors drop in for coffee and a chat; luncheons are arranged with friends you haven't seen in a while; meetings are organized; and of course the countless moments arise when you need to bandage a scraped knee, settle a quarrel between playmates, or hunt for that lost baseball glove.

Meal preparation is only one of the many daily demands of family life. Organization has to extend to every area, if this one particular aspect of your day is to be streamlined.

Here are some suggestions that may help:

- "Superwoman" is the stuff of comics books, not the everyday home. Don't waste your energies trying to be the best on the block.
- Avoid allowing unplanned activities to take a lot of your time. If a neighbor drops in, chat, but carry on with your work.
- Work according to your own inner time clock. Many of us work best in the morning, so that's the time to shop, cook, tidy, or whatever. Work when you know you'll be at

your peak, and save your most difficult
tasks for this time.

- Look for the tiny time wasters (sitting down
  with a cup of coffee in front of a TV show
  you don't *really* enjoy watching).
- Learn to say no. Don't agree to do things
  you don't want to do, or know you don't
  have time for.
- Don't put off tasks you know must be done.
  Procrastinating only increases tension, and
  that refrigerator that must be cleaned won't
  go away.
- Set a work time and a play time; then you
  won't feel guilty if you're enjoying a game
  of tennis, having left a sink full of dishes.
- Schedule a free evening or a free weekday
  to do just what you want. (Even a few hours
  is a help, at first.)
- Make up a "to do" list. Write down every
  household task that you want completed —
  from mending the wallpaper in the bed-
  room, to cleaning the basement. Discuss this
  with the family, and ask for "volunteers."
  Divide the jobs up.
- Be realistic. Don't invite friends over for
  dinner on the days you know you've got to
  take the kids to the dentist.
- Plan ahead to avoid this pitfall: "I haven't
  time to cook, so we'll all eat out." Have
  foods in the freezer for those extra-busy
  days. Or make a simple meal—you don't
  need all the trimmings each night.
- Remember, disorganization at home affects
  your relationship with your family, your so-

cial life, and your peace of mind.

To help organize meals and meal times—which can take a big chunk out of your day:

- Try to block time once a week to prepare foods that freeze well and reheat—casseroles and meatloaves. Double the quantity. A freezer is a great investment (small units are available for apartment dwellers). So's a microwave oven.
- Try to keep kitchen organization as simple as possible. Have you ever heard the expression that "a refrigerator is a holding tank for guilt"? What are you really going to do with that chicken wing, that dab of gravy, or the few tablespoons of mashed potatoes that have been there for a week? Unless leftovers are definitely planned for another meal, throw them out. It may seem like a waste at the time, but unless you're going to use them quickly, it's best not to keep them languishing.
- Talk to your family. Show them your "to do" list, and ask their help in planning the week's menus. You may find your teenager is delighted to help with some of the grocery shopping or cooking, and perhaps it can become a paid chore. Even young children like to help. Establish a job chart. A canvas wall hanging with big pouches can be filled with pictures of jobs to be done; toss in an extra treat or rewards (one extra story at bedtime?).
- If the kids tote their own lunch, have a Sun-

day evening sandwich-making bee. Make a
week's supply of favorites at one time and
freeze them (except that the least popular
are usually the only ones left each Friday).

MENU PLANNING

According to Brillat Savarin, the celebrated gastronome, a
well-planned menu is the secret of a successful meal. Although menu preparation takes time and practice, the
benefits are enormous. Menu planning is a definite pre-
requisite to a balanced and varied diet.

It isn't meal preparation that is usually the major
problem, but rather the daily decision of what to make. If
you only do this once a week, you'll save yourself headaches. Weekly planning helps simplify shopping, makes
use of leftovers, and takes advantage of advertised specials.
Also, think about lunches to be taken to work or school.
While you may not stick to the menu exactly, knowing you
have everything you need in the kitchen will be a big relief.

Many factors must be kept in mind when planning
menus: the nutritional value of various foods, the budget,
the time of year, your family's individual likes and dislikes, as well as the age and activity of family members.
How much time do you have to prepare foods—and what is
your kitchen equipment like?

Post your meal plans prominently in the kitchen.
Plan your shopping list around them. They're also good
reminders to you to thaw any frozen food you need. And
encourage your husband or children to start dinner if they
get home first.

To plan your menus, devise a general plan that suits
your family. For example, for lunch or dinner include:

- A protein food. This may be meat, eggs, milk, or mixed vegetable proteins. It may be the main course or part of a casserole, a stir-fried combination, a stew, or other mixed dish.
- One or more raw or cooked green or yellow vegetables. Two vegetables similar in flavor, such as cabbage and cauliflower, shouldn't be used at the same meal. We eat with our eyes too, so vary the shape of the vegetables and arrange them attractively.
- Complex carbohydrates for the majority of calories. This can be bread, potatoes, pasta, rice, corn, or other starchy cereal or vegetable. While the potato has been a main food in North America, some of the others take less time and effort to prepare.

Desserts, if used at all, should complement the main course. An egg-, cheese- or milk-based dessert, or fresh or processed fruit, are good nutritional choices. To round out your menu, start with or include a salad or soup. (Don't serve a cream soup and milk-based dessert at the same meal.)

You don't have to follow this pattern all the time, of course. For example, if your family normally has light cereal-and-juice breakfasts, a heavier breakfast of a ham omelet, fruit salad, rye, or other special toast can be served for supper on a busy night. Breakfasts and snacks should also be planned to supply the essential nutrients. The choice of beverage is up to you, although milk is essential for children.

Once you've finished planning, check the aesthetic, nutritional, and economic merits of the menus. Are a variety of cooking methods used? Are contrasts in colors, flavors, or textures used?

Here's a very basic outline for each meal of the day.

BREAKFAST
Fruit, fruit juice, or tomato juice
Whole grain or refined cereal with milk *or*
Bread or muffins with cheese
Meat or alternatives, if desired

LUNCH AND DINNER
Soup or Juice
Meat or alternatives
Cooked or raw vegetables
Bread, potatoes, rice, or other such food
Fruit or dairy-based dessert

ECONOMIZING

Time is not the only problem. We have to be more and more concerned about the price we have to pay for food. While soaring food prices make new headlines at least once a month, North Americans spend only about sixteen to seventeen percent of their budgets on food. In contrast, France spends about twenty percent of disposable income on food; Sweden, about twenty-four percent; the United Kingdom, about twenty-eight percent; and Finland, about thirty-four percent.

But we can't afford to be complacent. Agriculture Canada predicts that retail food prices will continue to rise about twelve to thirteen percent a year. Yet these higher prices may actually be good for us nutritionally. It may force us to become wiser shoppers. Many of us now cut back on the extras such as snacks, and use fewer convenience products to try to cope with inflation. We are also eating more salads, green vegetables, fresh fruit, and poultry (which is lower in fat content than most meat). Higher prices might force us to try to cut down on total food intake and, as a result, we may even lose a little weight.

You must get more for your food dollar. But more what? If all you needed was energy (calories), then a diet of lard and sugar might be most economical. If you only needed vitamins and minerals, you could gulp down pills. However, we don't recommend either solution.

First, we still don't know absolutely everything about the nutrients we need, particularly the trace minerals — that is, those we need or may need in very tiny amounts. These trace minerals aren't added to vitamin-mineral pills, but can be easily obtained in a diet with a wide variety of foods. Second, you're going to have to eat food anyway, for energy and protein. And finally, eating food is far more interesting than swallowing pills.

How can you get the most for your food dollar (and not spend too much time on planning and work)?

Plan your week's menus, referring to weekly food advertisements to determine the best buys. Consider your family's likes and dislikes. Clip discount coupons for foods you really need. File these in a small box so you can check them before shopping. But beware. Sometimes one brand, even with a coupon, may be more expensive than another equally acceptable brand.

Prepare a grocery list before you go shopping — and stick to it. Stores are designed to tempt you! That's why milk, a staple, is always at the back of a store. The foods you buy on impulse are likely to be the most expensive and least nutritious. Avoid fancy packages and advertising gimmicks (such as premiums and games). Both add to the cost. Be suspicious of dramatic food displays. Don't assume they mean that the item is on sale.

Limit shopping trips to no more than once a week,

because it's those quick, frequent dashes to the supermarket that add up in dollars; you're more susceptible to "impulse buys." You don't even have to shop more often for milk. Keep an emergency supply of sterilized milk on hand. It contains all the nutrients of fresh milk and will keep unrefrigerated for several months. For an almost-fresh taste, open the carton and let it chill in the refrigerator a while before using.

Never shop on an empty stomach! Your stomach can be more powerful than your brain, and you'll go home with a lot of high-calorie, high-priced goodies you don't need.

Buy food in quantity, particularly staples if you have storage space and cash on hand. Stock up on good buys of canned and frozen products your family enjoys when they're on special. But limit your purchases of perishable foods to amounts your family will use before it spoils. Always check the "best before" date on perishable products to judge the food's freshness.

Other saving tips:

- Shop the "fitness-conscious" way. Lower-priced products are often placed on shelves below or above eye level, and a little bending and stretching may be worth the effort.
- Compare costs and buy food in the form (fresh, canned, or frozen) that gives the most servings for your dollar. Compare prices of various brand names, as advertised brands are often more expensive. Try the generic and house brands. Some are similar in quality to widely known brand names, yet cost less.

- Use foods in season and, if possible, freeze or process fresh produce available then, for use in winter.
- Calculate unit pricing to find the size of container that costs the least per unit. Buy yourself a small calculator to take shopping. You'll be surprised how often a bargain is not a bargain when you calculate unit cost.
- Look for day-old bread or baked products, usually offered by bakeries or supermarkets at sizeable reductions. Select cuts of meat and poultry that provide the most cooked "lean" for the dollar. Buy cheese in large wedges or sticks, often less expensive than grated or sliced.
- Unsweetened cereals are often less expensive than presweetened (and you can control the content of sugar you add). Cereals you cook yourself are usually far cheaper.
- Read labels. Ingredients are listed in decreasing order of content. Be wary of those which list sugar or other sweeteners as the first ingredient.

At home:

- Cut down on meat portion sizes. We don't need large chops, steaks, or hamburger patties. Fill the plate with vegetables and cereal products instead. They contain bulk, which makes you feel less hungry, and also supply vitamins and minerals.
- Try having one or more meatless days each

week. Use eggs, milk products, and recipes
that include beans, peas, and cereals to give
you all the protein you need.

- Take a second look at skim milk powder,
and use it for cooking or drinking.
- Cut back on fats and sweets (and, yes, alcohol), which mainly provide calories and
little in the way of nutrients.
- Prevent food waste and conserve nutrients
by proper storage and cooking methods.
- Avoid unnecessary leftovers (unless you
plan to use them later) by preparing foods
only in amounts needed.
- Save fuel by planning complete oven meals
and baking only one or two days a week,
rather than each day.

One of the best ways to ensure you and your family
get all the nutrients needed is to follow our old stand-by of
Canada's Food Guide or the *Basic Four* in the United
States, in which basic foods are listed in four groups. Selecting according to these food guide patterns will supply
about 1,200 to 1,400 calories a day, which is fine for most
women. If you're trying to lose weight, select the least
number of servings recommended and the lowest calorie
foods in that group (skim milk instead of homo, low-fat
cheese instead of creamed, spinach instead of corn).

Here are more savings suggestions for individual
foods:

Bread and cereals are high in the B vitamins and iron
needed by most women. They are a great source of fiber,
and are high in complex carbohydrates. When it's on special, buy bread that's 100% whole grain for best food
value—and freeze as many loaves as possible. If your

family doesn't eat a lot of bread, just take out a few frozen slices from a loaf the night before. Bread won't go moldy that way. (If it does go stale, cut it into thin slices and toast in a low-temperature oven for home-made melba toast, or cut into cubes for stuffing or croutons and buzz in the blender, along with a few herbs, for seasoned bread-crumbs.) Buy day-old bread as well, and check out bakery outlets in your community. Why not make old-fashioned bread puddings from time to time for dessert? They are a nice change from cakes and pies—and are lower in sugar.

Comparison shop. Check weight and number of slices per loaf. Sometimes sandwich bread costs less per serving because slices are thinner. Watch out for the so-called "diet" breads. They're usually more expensive and simply offer thinner slices.

Presweetened cereals are often more expensive. Stick to rolled oats, shredded wheat and bran cereals. Try adding wheat germ to cereals, or when you're baking. This isn't necessary if you're sure your family is already eating enough whole grains, but it gives waffles, pancakes, and other products an interestingly different taste.

Brown *rice* is your best nutrition buy. Then comes regular white, converted... and instant. Avoid the boxed, flavored rices. They're expensive when you figure out cost per serving. It's just as easy to add your own chicken or beef cubes to rice, or whatever herbs and spices you like.

Pasta is not fattening by itself (again, it's back to quantity—and how much cream, sauce, meat you add). Enriched pasta is an excellent source of B vitamins and iron. Plain-shaped pasta is less expensive than the fancy bows, ringlets, and other shapes (and tastes just as good).

Milk and milk products provide calcium, protein, and important vitamins such as A, D, and riboflavin. Skim milk powder is your best and cheapest source of nutrients from this group. Serve it icy cold, or mix it with 2% or skim milk, if you must. But substitute it for regular milk in all your recipes; in baking, puddings, sauces.

Add skim milk powder to casseroles and cooked cereals to increase nutrient value. And if your kids don't get quite as much milk as they should, make the powdered milk a little more concentrated by increasing the proportion of powder to liquid.

Fluid skim milk and 2% cost less than whole milk, yet contain all the same nutrients, except that the fat content is lower. Buttermilk can be a refreshing change and has the same calories as skim milk—about ninety calories in eight ounces (or 250 mL). And make your own flavored milk (the popular commercial flavored ones are high in sugar, and hence, calories). Simply add small amounts of cocoa.

Making your own *yoghurt* can be fun—and quite cheap. (Recipes are available through local health centers). Watch the sales on prepared yoghurt and stock up, because it keeps well in the refrigerator. Buy plain yoghurt and add your own fresh fruit (lower in sugar and price). Save the small containers; buy in large containers to economize, and if kids carry it to school, add it to the smaller containers yourself. Compare prices of frozen yoghurt with ice cream. Yoghurt is usually lower in fat content—but read the labels carefully. Substitute it for sour cream in dips or sauces; it's lower in fat and cost.

Cheese made in North America is usually less expensive than imported—and tastes great. Canadian cheddar cheese is known internationally. And Canadian Brie, in our opinion, holds its own against the French!

Check prices of bulk cheese *vs.* prepackaged or individually wrapped cheese. Grate your own cheddar or parmesan. It's cheaper and can be done easily by hand or with a blender. Grated cheese retains its texture when it is stored in the refrigerator in a tightly sealed jar to which you've added a sugar cube.

Use hardened cheese (cut in chunks or grated) in soups, casseroles. Make Welsh rarebits for nutritious and fairly low-cost lunches (double the batch, it freezes well). Brick cheese doesn't freeze well—but if you've bought in bulk, go ahead and freeze it for use in sauces and casseroles. If you have time, why not try making your own cheese spread?

HOME-MADE CHEESE SPREAD
Makes 2 lbs. (1 kg)
2 tbsp. (30 mL) margarine or butter
1 lb. (500 g) cheese (processed makes a
smoother spread)
2 egg yolks, beaten
1-13 oz. (385 mL) can evaporated milk
1 tbsp. (15 mL) flour

In a double boiler, melt butter and add cheese. When softened, add egg yolks, milk, and flour. Cook until thick. Place in a covered jar and refrigerate. This spread can be kept for up to two months.

(Courtesy of Saskatchewan Health)

Whipped dessert toppings and coffee whiteners are expensive and are *not* substitutes for milk products. Both are high in palm oil (saturated fats) and sugar.

Fruit and vegetables supply vitamins A and C as well as some calcium and iron. Buy in bulk from farm outlets, or markets in the summer when prices are lowest. Freeze or can as much as possible. Fresh fruit in winter is usually too expensive, so use the canned or frozen for a few months, rather than imported fresh produce. Over-ripe fruit can be puréed and frozen; even bananas can be used this way for quick breads.

Buy canned fruits that are packed in water rather than in heavy syrups. You'll save money and calories. Use diced or chopped fruits (the least expensive) if appearance isn't important. Buy standard grades. They're just as tasty and nutritious as the higher-priced "Fancy" or "Choice" grades.

Watch for specials, and use coupons. Large bags of frozen vegetables are cheaper than small packages. Add your own butter, sauces, and seasonings. And don't throw nutrition down the drain. Use a minimum amount of water to cook vegetables. Use any water left over in stews, soups, and casseroles.

In winter, experiment with cabbage for salads, rather than lettuce. Any good cookbook will give you lots of ideas. Bean sprouts are great for salads. Stretch your dollar by using them in numerous ways.

Meat and meat alternatives provide protein, B vitamins, and iron. One quick way to save is to cut back on portion sizes. We only need about three ounces of meat *daily*. So an eight-ounce steak is definitely out. Stir-frying is "in." This is a great way to cut back on the amount of meat you use while experimenting with unusual vegetable and flavor combinations.

Become your own butcher: cube meat for stews, casseroles; debone chickens, or cut up whole chickens; grind up leftovers for shepherd's pie, Cornish pastries. Freeze meat on special in recipe-sized portions. Buy in bulk when it's economical. But before you buy half a cow, make sure you really understand what cuts you're buying. Does your family like some of the more unusual cuts? If not, you may not have made as good a buy as you think. One consumer group put their supposed "half a cow" back together again and found they had a very abnormal animal! Know your supplier, or you may pay for extra bone and fat.

Less tender cuts are usually less expensive. They also have less fat and more protein per serving than higher grades. Marinating, or cooking in a clay-baker or crock pot, will tenderize. Use shoulder rather than rib or loin chops, blade or chuck steaks instead of T-bones. Try a "three-way" roast. Buy a prime rib on special and ask the butcher to remove the filet (for a special treat), trim the end (to grind for meatloaf) and bone and roll the remainder for a Sunday roast.

Chicken livers are cheap and delicious. Try to eat liver once a week. And experiment with interesting "variety" meats; hearty oxtail soups, glazed tongue, or stuffed heart are economical, tasty dishes.

Choose regular ground beef (up to thirty percent fat) for dishes like chili where the meat will be browned first and then the fat drained off. Use leaner ground beef (more expensive) for meatloaves, patties.

Plan at least one meatless meal a week. Combine legumes (beans, peas, lentils) with whole grains, seeds, or nuts to equal a complete protein food (see p. 170).

We should eat more *fish and poultry*, not only because they are economical, but because they're lower in fat and calories. Buy larger sized poultry and freeze leftovers for sandwiches, soups, casseroles. Fish is a particularly good buy. One pound should be ample for three to four people. "Chuck" and flaked fish is cheaper than solid-pack, but is equal in nutrition. Unless appearance matters, buy pink rather than sockeye red salmon. And substitute mackerel for tuna and salmon from time to time.

FAST FOODS

Why not make your own "fast food"—and make it more nutritious!

A plain hot dog contains some protein, iron, and B vitamins. It's not too high in calories—about 135. Add diced tomatoes, warmed processed cheese spread, or a strip of cheddar cheese in the middle for calcium ... or baked beans for a "chili dog," to provide such nutrients as protein, vitamins, and iron. Even sauerkraut (which is low in calories) will give you some vitamins A and C, and iron. So will processed cheese spread, melted in a microwave or under the broiler.

A plain hamburger and an enriched or whole wheat roll gives you about half of your daily protein needs, some B vitamins, and a lot of iron, as well as carbohydrates, for under 200 calories. Add a cheese slice to a hamburger to provide calcium, lettuce and tomatoes for vitamins A and C, bean sprouts or beans for extra vitamins and minerals.

A medium slice of pizza with tomato and cheese sauce is chock full of protein, calcium, vitamins A, C, and B, and carbohydrates—and has only about 200 calories. Add green peppers for more A and C, anchovies for calcium and protein, mushrooms, which are low-calorie, lean cooked beef, or sliced meat for protein.

Here are three recipes for time-conscious penny-pinchers (courtesy of Saskatchewan Health).

CHOW MEIN   Serves 6-8
*1 lb. (500 g) pork, beef, or chicken, cut in thin
slices*

3 cups (750 mL) celery, sliced diagonally
2 cups (500 mL) onions, sliced
1 cup (250 mL) green pepper, sliced
3 cups (750 mL) fresh bean sprouts
¼ tsp. (1 mL) powdered ginger
1 tsp. (5 mL) sugar
3 tbsp. (45 mL) cornstarch
5 tbsp. (75 mL) soy sauce
¼ cup (60 mL) soup stock
1 tbsp. (15 mL) oil

Combine ginger, sugar, cornstarch, soy sauce, and soup stock and set aside. Heat oil in large skillet, add meat, and stir-fry just until done. Remove from skillet.

Stir-fry vegetables (except sprouts) in 1 tbsp. (15 mL) oil until tender crisp. Return meat to skillet. Add sauce and sprouts. Cook until sauce thickens and serve.

Dairy products, eggs, and vegetable proteins are a good substitute for meat and are much less expensive.

EGG BURGER   Serves 1
1 tsp. (5 mL) margarine or butter
1 egg
salt and pepper
grated or sliced cheese
1 whole wheat bun, toasted

Melt margarine in frying pan over moderate heat. Break egg into pan. With a pancake-turner, break egg yolk and mix with egg white. Sprinkle with salt and pepper. Finely chopped green onion, green peppers, mushrooms, or leftovers may be sprinkled on egg at this stage of cooking.

When egg is set, turn and cook other side. Place cheese on top of egg, then transfer to the warm bun. Serve at once.

Vegetables are an important source of vitamins and minerals in our diet, but often receive little or no planning when it comes to meal time. Teach your family to become "vegetable addicts" by frequently serving vegetables raw and *never* overcooked.

STIR-FRIED BROCCOLI AND
CAULIFLOWER   Serves 4-5
½ cup (125 mL) chicken broth
1 tsp. (5 mL) cornstarch
2 tbsp. (30 mL) soy sauce
1 tsp. (5 mL) sugar
3 tbsp. (45 mL) oil
½ medium onion, diced
½ lb. (250 g) broccoli, cut in small pieces
½ lb. (250 g) cauliflower, cut in small pieces
2 tbsp. (30 mL) sesame seeds

Combine broth, cornstarch, soy sauce, and sugar. Set aside. Heat oil in large skillet. Add onion, stir-fry until golden. Add broccoli and cauliflower. Stir-fry for three minutes. Add sauce ingredients. Stir-fry for one minute until sauce clears. Sprinkle with sesame seeds and serve.

SMART COOKING

Let's look at an example of a typical family Sunday dinner.

Tossed green salad, roast beef, mashed potatoes, mixed vegetables, white rolls, fruit—sure sounds like a nutritious meal you've just prepared. But perhaps it's not as nutritious as you first thought.

First of all, to save last-minute rushing you sliced all the salad vegetables in the morning. Then you peeled off the outer leaves of the lettuce and soaked the inner leaves in ice water to keep them crisp. You took the roast out of the freezer in the morning to let it defrost. You not only peeled the potatoes but cooked and mashed them, ready for reheating. After thawing the mixed vegetables slightly, you boiled and drained them.

These routine meal preparation techniques lead to significant nutrient loss. How many errors did you recognize?

Nutrient losses begin at the time food products are harvested. Although many people feel that industrial processing is the major offender, extensive nutrient losses occur at home in the kitchen—in the refrigerator, down the sink, or on the stove. Micronutrients (vitamins and minerals) are the greatest concern. These are the principal nutrients that may be needlessly lost by faulty home preparation.

First of all, it's best to scrub but not peel vegetables, and to slice them just prior to serving and cooking. Soaking the lettuce and discarding the outer leaves results in nutrient loss. Cook potatoes in the skin prior to peeling. This not only helps retain nutrients but increases the amount of fiber. Steam frozen vegetables in a covered pot until tender and crisp (never thaw frozen vegetables before cooking). A nutritionally wise practice: save any vegetable water and use it as a stock in soups and gravies. But use as little water as possible when cooking vegetables.

It's also wise to cook the roast from the frozen state

and re-use the meat drippings, as thawing meat may result
in a considerable loss of protein, B vitamins, and minerals,
all found in the discarded juices. (Trimming the fat is a
wise practice in terms of calories, even though some nutrient losses may occur.)

Last but not least, serve whole wheat rolls, not white.
Whole grain flour supplies more of the B-complex vitamins and minerals than white. Enrichment of white flour
replaces only some of the nutrients removed during
milling.

Loss of fat-soluble vitamins (vitamins A, D, E, K) is
usually minimal during food preparation. But water-
soluble vitamins can be lost in preparation as they tend to
get thrown out with the cooking water. Vitamin C and thiamin are the most easily destroyed by heating. As a rule, if
you follow precautions to achieve optimum vitamin C and
thiamin during food preparation—for example, using the
minimum amount of water and cooking quickly whenever
possible—most other nutrients are also retained.

Food storage can be an additional cause of nutrient
loss. Store foods for no longer than three months in a refrigerator freezer compartment. Your freezer should be set
at -18°C (0°F) or lower. Freezing is a good method of pre-
serving the nutritive value of vegetables and fruits following proper blanching, adequate packaging, and then rapid
freezing.

Vegetables should be stored in plastic bags or crispers
in the refrigerator. Produce shouldn't be washed or trim-
med prior to storage. Canned fruits and vegetables should
be stored in a cool place, 15°C (59°F) or cooler, for maximum vitamin retention. The packing juice will then contain nutrients, so don't throw it down the drain. Dried
fruits and vegetables are higher in vitamins if proper con-

trols are used. Sun-drying can cause spoilage and vitamin losses. While the new commercial dryers now on the market are designed to ensure optimum nutrient retention, caution must be used. Dry heat and circulating air can cause nutrient losses. Therefore, home-dried products may have minimal vitamin value.

Of course, it's impossible to get the optimum for every nutrient at each meal; some of our food preparation practices are for convenience. But a few precautions can prevent needless loss of those nutrients.

6 The Career Woman

As women are moving quickly up the ladder of success, they're bound to face unfamiliar stresses and may experience certain health problems as a result. And you don't have to have the key to the executive washroom to suffer from some of these problems. It can happen to any woman who is juggling a life away from home with a life *at* home. You may start suffering from "role-overload"—trying to do too much, trying to be too many things to too many people, simply trying to fill too many roles.

Today's female executive has to look and feel her best from 9:00 to 5:00 (and often after) in this increasingly competitive world. If you want to look and feel great, an awareness of proper nutrition and eating habits is essential.

Rapid changes in the business world have expanded the opportunities for women. Your state of "wellness," both physical and mental, is thus going to be of prime importance. (If you're a boss, you have even more reason to be health-conscious. With mounting and costly employee absenteeism due to illness, and rising health expenditures, be concerned about your employees' present state of health, and about how they're going to stay healthy.)

If you're working harder and enjoying it less because of such work-related hazards as stress, weight gain, hypertension, cardiovascular (heart) disease and fatigue—all quite probable concerns for those in the work force—read on.

Female heroes emulated over the years have included the Bette Davis type, cigarette dangling from one corner of her mouth, or Twiggy, with her bone-sharp lack of curves, or Liz Taylor, dripping with diamonds, a glass of champagne in her hand. The only people hooked on natural foods were the Greta Garbos and the Gloria Swansons, and they were considered to be a bit of an oddity. Then along came the natural craze, and shots of famous women like Jane Fonda, Barbra Streisand, even Bo Derek, that told all—they jog, swim, exercise, eat properly, don't smoke, and very seldom drink. They practically glow with good vibrations. Female athletes state that they get their highs from running; once they've reached a certain distance, a sense of tranquility pervades their senses and they run to the beat of a different drummer.

We are now a health-conscious society. Just look around you at the no-smoking signs that abound everywhere, from taxis to elevators to airplanes to posh (and not so posh) restaurants. The new "in" drinks are Perrier — and sugarless iced tea with mint.

Many corporations and some major hospitals offer fitness programs to their executives and staff. Some major corporate giants have on-site gyms. Others offer full or partial membership in a nearby health spa. And a few hotels offer fitness weekends.

Upwardly mobile female executives who know it pays to look and feel their best escape to health spas in the country. Here they receive expert nutrition and fitness counseling. (Such programs are offered in the United States, but they're pricey. Call your local "Y" or health unit to see if there are any recommended in your area.)

In fashion, the jogging suit in marvelously bright colors has replaced basic black and pearls as a status symbol. And spike-heeled shoes are looked upon scornfully while the pros and cons of the eighty different styles of running shoes are hotly discussed at coffee breaks. One major department store has enlarged its sporting goods more than thirty-five percent and intends to continue expanding. Nutrition has become as topical as the best way to correct a golf swing or handle a squash racquet.

Why? Because we're rediscovering something our grandparents practiced when they toiled in the fields and ate nourishing foods. It's called a life style, or holistic living. The emphasis is on prevention, rather than cure. And that's great. If you're healthy now, try to *stay* that way. Executives, along with everyone else, are beginning to realize that *they* have the responsibility for their own bodies; no magic gizmo or diet will do it for them.

REDUCING HEALTH RISKS

Women's increasing presence in the work place is exacting

a price. We may have higher self-esteem, solid rights, and more independence, but we're also coping with the negative aspects of corporate life: stress and its effects on our health. Our society has emphasized, in former years, the need to look after our "menfolk," to make sure they eat well and exercise enough so that the risk of *heart attack* is reduced.

But women are vulnerable too. Women tend to have fewer heart attacks than men, but we can't develop a false sense of security. (Women who suffer a heart attack are twice as likely to suffer a second attack within five years, according to the American Heart Association.) The prognosis for women who have had an attack is far worse than for men; in fact, about forty-five percent of women die within a year of suffering the nonfatal attack (compared to only twenty percent of men).

For some women working outside the home, the risk of developing heart disease increases. A study found that single working women were less likely to have a heart attack than women who work at home. But the combination of demanding family life *and* a career increased the risk for some women. The study showed that working women who had raised three or more children had higher rates of heart disease than homemakers in otherwise comparable circumstances.

Until recently, nearly all studies linking psychosocial factors to heart disease involved only men. These studies suggest higher rates of heart disease occur among men who are hard-driving, ambitious, always in a hurry, and anxious for control of their situation.

Women have always had much lower rates of coronary heart disease than men, but many observers have predicted women would shed their protection as they entered the work force and faced the same stresses as men. Thus far, however, statistics have not borne this out. Coronary death rates have been dropping for both men and women in Canada and the United States in the last decade. And the decline has been greater for women, even though the proportion of women who work has increased enormously since 1950, so that now half of all women work outside the home. Even so, coronary heart disease is responsible for more than half of all deaths in North America and for one-third of all deaths among people under sixty-five.

If you have a history of heart disease or have been told by your doctor that you are a prime candidate, you'll want to read this section carefully. It contains a basic approach to prevention that will be useful even if you simply want to reduce your chances of developing heart disease.

No one knows yet exactly why heart disease develops. We do know that the likelihood of having heart problems is associated with certain risk factors. These include high levels of certain fats (cholesterol and triglycerides) in the blood, high blood pressure, diabetes, and perhaps smoking. Overweight itself is not a major factor unless you also have high blood pressure. Stress and lack of exercise are also important risk factors.

But what about your diet? What can you eat—or not eat—that may lessen your chances of having a heart attack? The American Heart Foundation and the Canadian government have issued some guidelines that make good nutrition sense. The American system is often referred to as the "prudent diet"—that is, following these recommendations won't guarantee a sound heart and blood system, but current studies indicate that they're likely to be significantly helpful. The recommendations are:

- stay close to the "ideal" weight
  (see the tables on page 154)
- cut down total fat intake
- cut down on the amount of saturated fat and
  cholesterol
- reduce your intake of salt

More than half the people in North America are carrying around more weight than they should. Toting a twenty-pound piece of baggage wherever you go obviously puts an unnecessary strain on your heart; extra body weight means extra effort too, and *that* you can do without! Keep in mind, too, that overweight people are more likely to have diabetes, high blood pressure, and high blood fat levels (cholesterol and triglycerides); all of these are risk factors in heart disease. We'll discuss practical approaches to integrating weight control into your busy schedule later in the chapter.

More and more medical research, done on a continuing basis, confirms the relationship between high levels of fats called cholesterol and triglycerides in your blood and the thickening of the arterial walls that's known as atherosclerosis. How does cholesterol get into your blood stream? Your body manufactures a certain amount for specific needs; the rest comes from what you eat. The amount of cholesterol you absorb from your diet depends on how much and what kind of fat you eat.

The two basic types of fat are saturated and polyunsaturated. The first comes mainly from animal fats, the second from most foods of vegetable origin. *Cut back on your total fat intake, especially on the saturated or animal fats.* Fat should make up no more than thirty percent of your total daily energy (on the average we now get over forty percent of our calories from fat.) No more than ten percent should come from animal sources — as compared to the present fifty to seventy percent we get. A juicy twelve-ounce steak makes a great dinner, but it gives you more than three times the recommended daily intake of protein, plus a lot of unwanted calories and saturated fats!

Keep this in mind when planning your diet:

- Avoid high levels of saturated fats, found in pork, beef, veal, egg yolks, whole milk, cream, ice cream, olive and coconut oils, and solid vegetable shortening. Polyunsaturated fats, which are preferable, are found in fish, liquid vegetable oils and margarines made from corn, soybean or safflower bases — and from your old friend peanut butter.

High blood pressure (hypertension) is one of the risk factors for heart disease. And between seventeen and twenty-five percent of North Americans have high blood pressure. Hypertension can be caused by a number of factors. In some people, one of these factors is sodium intake. Sodium is a nutrient, and an essential one, but too much may cause water retention and hypertension.

The exact amount of sodium we need hasn't yet been established, but one to three grams a day seems to be sufficient for most adults. That's equal to about three to eight grams of salt. Instead, we usually consume ten to twelve grams a day. We add twenty-five to fifty percent of the salt we eat to our foods. Another major source is processed foods — which also may contain sodium compounds such as sodium phosphate or citrate. Even many drugs have a sodium base (a common bubbly antacid contains 276 mg of sodium per tablet). Some carbonated beverages are made with sodium bicarbonate. Others made with carbon dioxide may have no sodium.

We recommend that you reduce your total salt intake, especially if you or members of your family have high blood pressure. As a start, limit the amount of salt you use in cooking and at the table. Try lemon juice, sprinkled on vegetables after cooking, for a refreshing change. Experiment with herbs and spices for all sorts of new and delightful tastes. Also check labels for salt and sodium compounds in food, and try some of the newer low-salt products on the market.

Cut back on your alcohol intake. Alcohol, if it's overused, has been shown to build up fatty tissue in the liver — and that's not beneficial to your general state of health. In some people, the daily use of alcohol also increases the level of blood triglycerides. Alcohol has not been blamed for leading directly to heart disease. It can, however, contribute to your weight problem by stimulating your appetite — not to mention the extra calories it provides.

Don't count on vitamin E supplements. Although vitamin E is needed and used by the body, its role in the prevention of heart disease has not yet been conclusively proved. The amount of vitamin E needed by the body depends on age, sex, and diet; for adults it's 10-12 I.U. a day. You can include this vitamin in your diet if you make a point of eating whole grains, wheat germ, margarine, and leafy green vegetables with salad oil every day.

And what about stress? Researchers believe that direct psychological stresses may increase the risk of heart disease in certain groups of working women. Those with the highest risk had a nonsupportive boss, kept angry feelings bottled up, and had limited opportunities to escape from jobs that yielded little satisfaction beyond a pay check. The dual conflict between home and job can cause heart-damaging stress.

The effect of stress may be direct. It may also affect what you choose to eat or drink. Both the stress and your response to it are likely to take their toll on your performance and your health. Stress can make you pick listlessly at food or nibble on all kinds of high-energy snacks. Yet you need to be in top form in order to cope with the pressure. Here are a few tricks.

If you're a worrier, you probably skip meals and don't pay much attention to what you eat. This can cause a nutritional imbalance. One study showed that students under stress of exams lost protein. Perhaps this happens to you as well. If you're too worried to eat because you have a job interview coming up, or an important presentation, or a big decision to make, the chances of meeting your nutritional needs are reduced. As a result, your body calls on its reserves—and you run the risk of depletion. When you know a "big moment" is coming up at work, try to include milk, fruit, vegetables, salads, and hefty whole wheat sandwiches. Meals don't have to be huge, sit-down affairs when you're a little on edge. Try eggnogs, munching on celery and carrot sticks, or a particular treat you really enjoy—like a cone with superflavored ice cream. It might even help take your mind off tomorrow's event.

Or if the reverse is true and stress causes you to want to nibble continuously, remember that overeating can make you feel drowsy and inattentive. And that's the last thing you need. Reach for some energizing snacks instead. Here are some under 100 calories: an apple, a handful of peanuts, a banana, a hard-boiled egg, a cup of hot bouillon, a few celery sticks stuffed with peanut butter, four or five crackers.

Coffee—countless cups—is like a crutch to some people when they're under stress. But the caffeine in coffee, tea, cola, and cocoa may cause you to feel even more nervous and jittery if you drink too much. And forget those wake-up pills! Interestingly (but no positive proof as yet), that old adage about the glass of hot milk as a natural sedative is being challenged. It appears that protein (cheese, milk, meat) keeps you alert. So save the protein for the morning. At night nibble on some crackers or a wafer instead.

There seems to be no end to the "help" you can get for stress through the high-powered (?) vitamins. One company promotes three vitamin packs, one for women, one for athletes, and one for stress victims. Presumably if you happen to be athletic, a woman, and under stress, you are meant to pop all of these. Watch out—you may be in for an overdose of vitamins, and for a large, expensive daily habit.

Actually there is no evidence that stress—real or imagined—directly increases the need for nutrients. If you're not eating properly (and we hope you'll change that), your diet may be low in nutrients and a supplement might help. But these megavitamins act as a placebo; that is, you feel better just because you believe you will. "Super-vitamins" do not lead to superhealth. Using such pills lures you into believing that you no longer need to be concerned about what you eat. Pills should be only supplements, never a replacement for balanced eating.

CONTROLLING YOUR WEIGHT

Being overweight isn't just a matter of looks. It's a real health hazard. It increases the risk of diabetes, gall bladder problems, hypertension, and heart disease in later years. It complicates pregnancy and surgery and may cause respiratory difficulties.

But, all too often we hear the "working woman's lament." "How can I keep my weight under control? With my travel schedule—eating on the run, business lunches, dinners and cocktail parties—there's no time left to 'touch my toes.' Who can exercise or watch their weight with those kinds of professional demands?" The answer—you can. The office life style does pose its own set of problems, but there are just as many solutions.

First, read Chapter 7 for a general discussion of fitness and the basic approach to weight control. Then continue on in this chapter for personalized tips about integrating weight control with the "prudent diet" and your special life style. The approach is simple:

- Eat more fruit, vegetables, and whole grains.
- Eat less fatty meats such as beef and pork and more lean meats like veal.
- Include fish and poultry in your diet.
- Cut down on sugar and high-sugar items.
- Substitute skim or 2% milk for whole milk.
- Cut down on foods high in fat. Substitute polyunsaturated fat when possible.
- Cut down on eggs, butterfat, and other high-cholesterol foods.
- Reduce the amount of salt you use, and cut down on foods already high in salt—bacon, salted nuts, and so on.
- Cut down on alcohol consumption.

The application may not be as easy. It's maddening, frustrating, and difficult to try to change your diet and/or lose weight at the best of times. The corporate woman requires real juggling skill to eat on the run, travel, entertain—and perhaps keep up with her professional peers at the current favorite watering-hole. It's a matter of trade-offs; remember that size ten tailored suit, rather than the loose-fitting, no-style tent dress. You must make your own choices. Armed with the desire, and some common-sense advice on how to handle the social pressures of eating, you can reach your goal.

NINE TO FIVE

Let's look at a normal business day. An 8:00 a.m. meeting has been called. You know coffee will be available. And at the last meeting, sticky, gooey Danishes from the office cart were offered.

Should you: sleep in an extra few minutes, knowing that there'll be food available? Get up a few minutes early and have a small glass of juice, some whole grain cereal and milk—perhaps an ounce of cheese? Skip breakfast because you know you'll be able to resist the temptation of the Danish? Or do you offer to pick up some bran muffins on your way to work? The choice is yours.

Don't be a breakfast skipper. It doesn't work. Many people think that because they're on a diet they can skip the first meal of the day and hang on until lunch. Don't skip *any* meal if you're dieting. Include some protein at breakfast—a hunk of hard cheese, a hard-boiled egg, even a small piece of chicken or other cold meat. You'll find that proteins help tide you over until the noon-hour even better than carbohydrates, and you won't get stuck with that dreaded disorder, the "tummy rumble," which always strikes as you are about to present your report or when there's a pregnant pause in the discussions. And most of us don't have enough willpower to pass up that donut or Danish if our stomachs are empty.

Turn coffee breaks into nutrition breaks. When the coffee cart comes by look for the small packages of cheese spread and crackers that are so popular now. They come in a few interesting flavors. Buy the can of juice or carton of milk rather than the coffee. If you must have a sweet from time to time, select the packages of oatmeal cookies, and just have half (fifty calories)—give the rest to your nondieting cohort.

There's no nutritional commandment that states you should only get your nutrients at 7:30 a.m., 12:00 noon, and 6:00 p.m.—just as long as you get them. The catch is that we're getting over thirty percent of our calories as snacks. Unfortunately the nutrient density (the amount of nutrients in 100 calories) of certain snack foods is lower than that of foods normally eaten at sit-down, family-style meals. That means you may be getting too many calories and being short-changed on nutrients as well. Give the same amount of thought and consideration to your snack foods as you do to the food you select at meals.

Snacking can be fine in moderation. It's been shown that calories eaten as several small meals over the course of the day are less likely to be changed into body fat than the same number of calories eaten during one or two large meals.

Photocopy the following list of low-calorie snacks. Keep one at home, and tack another (or frame it!) next to the picture of the kids on your office desk.

NUTRITIOUS NOSHES (ABOUT 100 CALORIES EACH)

1 medium banana
1½ cups (375 mL) fresh
  raspberries
¾ cup (200 mL) plain yoghurt
small baked custard
1 oz. (30 g) blue cheese
1 oz. (30 g) blue cheese spread
  plus 3 crackers
½ small liverwurst sandwich
small bowl beef noodle soup
9-12 mixed shelled nuts
small piece angel food cake
10 dill pickles
3 cups (750 mL) beef broth
½ cup (125 mL) oyster stew
  (made with milk)
4 thin pretzels
small slice pizza
1 cup (250 mL) plain
  cornflakes (no milk or
  sugar)
1½ slices whole wheat bread
2 tangerines
1 medium grapefruit
2 large fresh peaches
1 oz. (30g) Camembert cheese
1 plain cookie
6 soda crackers
½ oz. (15 g) sunflower seeds
small handful seedless raisins
⅔ lb. (1.4 kg) fresh bean
  sprouts
13 melba toast rounds
2 cups (500 mL) popcorn (oil
  added)
1 tbsp. (15 mL) peanut butter
1 glass fresh orange juice

1 wedge watermelon
2 slices crisp bacon
1 cup (250 mL) buttermilk
3 oz. (90 g) creamed cottage
  cheese
1 cup (250 mL) canned
  asparagus (solids and
  liquids)
5 uncooked prunes
1½ raw apples, medium
¼ avocado
2 raw tomatoes
1 cup (250 mL) blueberries
⅓ average size hamburger
  plus bun
⅓ cup (80 mL) sherbet
½ plain waffle
12 almonds
1 cup (250 mL) skim milk
2 cups (500 mL) tomato juice
3 cups (750 mL) green beans,
  raw
3 oz. (90 g) raw clams
2½ oz. (75 g) canned salmon,
  drained
1½ oz. (45 g) beef liver,
  broiled
1 slice bologna
1 medium baked or boiled
  potato, plain
6 tiny whole beets
2 whole stalks broccoli,
  cooked
10 cups (2500 mL) Chinese
  cabbage, raw
1 glass lemonade
4 fresh plums, small

(Don't forget that even if the snacks do contain only 100 calories each, ten or twelve of these can fill your entire day's calorie quota.)

NINE TO FIVE: LUNCHING OUT

There are a few simple tricks you can use to help yourself cope when you're eating at the nearby noshery.

First of all, tell your associates you're dieting. (Even just making the announcement commits you to ordering something low-cal.) Tell them that, come what may, you're going to stick to it. Enlist their support.

Then, when the first round of cocktails are ordered make yours soda with lime. (It's the prestigious "in" drink, anyway—and just think how alert *you'll* be at 2:30 that afternoon.)

Read the menu carefully. (We applaud those astute eating establishments that offer salad bars, list calories beside the various dishes, and offer a low-cal special of the day. In some restaurants, in California in particular, the cholesterol count of dishes is also included, and many exotic-sounding vegetarian dishes are offered, often lower in calories.) Head straight for the salad bar. Fill up on greens, bean salad, egg slices, grated cheese, but skip the potato, macaroni, corn—and the dressing. Ask for a wedge of lemon instead, or tote your own low-calorie version.

Order poached or broiled rather than fried dishes. Ask that the "meunière" or "amandine" on the sole be left off. (Steel yourself. You may offend the chef's sense of pride in culinary creation, but you're the one on the diet. Besides, the really progressive chefs are preparing more and more scrumptious low-energy dishes.) Avoid sauced dishes, for example, plain poached eggs, no eggs Benedict, please. Ask the waiter to substitute sliced tomatoes or green beans for higher energy peas and corn. Choose lean meats (veal, chicken, or fish). Remove the batter or skin from such deep-fried dishes as chicken or fish. Better still, don't order batter-fried foods in the first place.

Order a plain baked potato, and shake your head when the butter and sour cream are offered. Tell the waiter you do not want any gravy or sauce on your entrée. Order clear consommé, either hot or chilled, as a starter, or plain tomato juice.

And unless there's fresh fruit or some cheese available, no dessert. If you have a say in where you're going for lunch, or if you're doing the inviting, select a Japanese restaurant (try to entice your guest into learning the joys of chic sushi bars). French—including the *nouvelle cuisine*—and Italian restaurants can be murder. There are a number of vegetarian noshing spots now. Try them.

In a fast-food place try a single patty hamburger (remove half the bun) for 200 calories, one-half cup (125 mL) tomato juice (45 calories) and an apple (bring your own) at 90 calories: this will have a grand total of 335 calories. We're pleased that these places too are beginning to offer a wider variety of low-fat and low-calorie foods— broiled rather than fried fish, unsweetened fruit juices, even salad bars.

NINE TO FIVE: LUNCHING IN

More and more executives are brown-bagging it. It's become almost as much of a status symbol as the Cross pen. (One high-class German china manufacturer even has vases made in the shape of the brown bag.)

Brown-bagging is a boon for executive dieters (and in light of the passing of the $2 lunch, a good financial idea as well). Sandwiches needn't be boring. Here are a few tasty, nutritious, and low-energy suggestions:

> • a variety of hard cheeses and bread sticks, melba toast

- cold chicken or meatloaf
- tomato halves stuffed with egg salad
- tossed salad with ham and cheese or a spin-ach/bacon/mushroom salad with a lemon-herb dressing carried on the side (add a muffin, skim milk, or cheese)
- Build your own open-face sandwiches (lean beef with tomatoes and pickles), hard-boiled egg slices with capers, marinated tiny shrimps with dill. Use a variety of breads for the base—half a bagel, dark rye, or oatmeal for those needed B vitamins and fiber.
- Dress up the lean meat sandwich by adding shredded carrots or cabbage. Add bean or alfalfa sprouts, diced celery. Look for the new calorie-reduced meats.

If you know you've got the dry-cleaning to pick up, shoes to be repaired, or shopping to be done, and no time for a sit-down lunch, take a thermos of fruit nogs. In the morning, throw a small banana, one egg, one cup (250 mL) cold skim milk, and a dash of honey (225 calories) into the blender. You've covered three of the four food groups this way. Add a muffin (120 calories) or melba toast and you've got a nutrition-filled lunch that should keep you going un-til dinner. You don't always have to carry milk: some of the new tomato or clamato juice combinations in cans are more expensive, but they're a nice, nutritious change. Freeze them ahead of time and they'll help keep other foods chilled.

And pack some raw veggies—carrots, green pepper slices, mushrooms, radishes, turnips, cauliflower, broccoli, green beans to add crunch to lunch. Take some plain yo-ghurt for a dip and share with your office co-workers.

(Ever thought of organizing an office lunch pool?)

Fruit salads you've made yourself offer a change from the standard banana or orange. Dried fruit is good nutritionally, but watch the calories, and be sure you brush your teeth afterwards, or at least rinse!

A word of warning if you're brown-bagging it. Proper food-handling precautions should be observed; the old rule of keep hot foods hot and cold foods cold must be followed.

It's the protein foods that often cause the problem. Certain meats (chicken or turkey), fish, and eggs are culprits if they've been improperly stored or cooled. Freeze sandwiches (do a week's supply at a time). Sandwiches taken out of the freezer in the morning will thaw by lunch time. Or use corned beef, bologna, summer sausage, or cheese. They're safe bets. So is the new nonrefrigerated yoghurt.

Keep hot soups hot in a thermos. For cold foods, if there is no refrigerator at work, use a freezer gel, or fill an old margerine tub with water and freeze. (Make sure it's tightly sealed.)

AFTER OFFICE HOURS

Stopping at the favorite neighborhood watering hole after work is becoming just as much a tradition as the business lunch. During office hours, there's a lot of pressure— deadlines, meetings, reports to be presented. After 5:00 p.m., the phones cease ringing, and it's time to relax with cohorts. Usually this means an invitation to join the gang for a "quick one" around the corner. How does this fit into your new eating plan?

Alcohol is high in calories, too many drinks can lead to nutritional (and other) problems, and of course alcohol doesn't supply any essential nutrients. But a glass of wine may act as a relief from stress for some—so it boils down to controlling your drinking habits. If you've "saved" 100 calories during the day, then your calorie intake may allow you to have *one* glass of dry wine.

Here's a calorie-counter for alcohol and mixes:

AMOUNT	CALORIES
1 glass of beer—regular (12 oz. or 375 mL)	150
1 glass of dry red wine (4 oz. or 125 mL)	95
1 glass of dry white wine (4 oz. or 125 mL)	95
gin (1½ oz. or 45 mL)	100
vodka (1½ oz. or 45 mL)	100
scotch (1½ oz. or 45 mL)	100
rye (1½ oz. or 45 mL)	100
rum (1½ oz. or 45 mL)	100
1 glass of cola (12 oz. or 375 mL)	145
1 glass of gingerale (12 oz. or 375 mL)	115

If you feel you must join your colleagues for that one drink from time to time, order a spritzer—half wine, half soda water. (Keep filling the glass with the soda.) Once that is gone, it's plain old soda with ice again.

The other problem associated with after-hours drinking is the plate of peanuts, chips, and pretzels that magically appears. (Salty snacks tend to make you thirsty, and they're great for the bartender's profits.) Again, if you really think you can stop after those four pretzels (100 calories), and you have the calories coming to you, fine. But we suggest taking the tempting dish to another table, or putting it as far away from you as possible. Keep the chart in mind. (If you must, four pretzels have fewer calories than a handful of peanuts.)

If you're entertaining at home, write away for a copy

of Health and Welfare Canada's *Great Entertainers*, available free of charge from Health and Welfare Canada, Health Protection Branch, Ottawa, Ontario, Canada, K1A 0C6. It's full of smashing "cocktail" recipes—without the booze. But be cautious; many are high in sugar. Here are two great cocktail ideas from the book.

.   MOONLIGHT COCKTAIL
    Shake ¾ cup (175 mL) canned or fresh grapefruit juice with ½ tsp. (2 mL) grenadine and crushed ice. Pour into an old-fashioned glass. Add short straws and a slice of lime on side of glass.

    BITTER-SWEET COCKTAIL
    Shake ¼ cup (60 mL) strong tea, 2 tbsp.(30 mL) fresh orange juice, and a dash of Angostura bitters with crushed ice. Strain into small cocktail glass. Garnish with a cocktail cherry and a lemon twist.

Remember, it's not only the calories in the booze, but in the mixers. Check your calorie book and you'll see how the calories double when mixers are added. Stick to soda or plain water for mixed drinks.

TRAVELING

Traveling on business can play havoc with a diet. Be prepared when you set out, and you can forestall extra calories.

If you know you'll be flying during a meal period, check with the airline first. Most airlines offer diabetic or low-cholesterol menus as well as items low in calories. But you must ask for this service at the time of booking and should identify yourself to the flight attendant when you board. (Special meals are often better than the regular ones.)

With more and more airlines trying to cut costs, meals will not be served on short hops, or even on longer flights that coincide with meal time. You may find yourself starving, so that you head for the first food available after you land. To combat this fast-food syndrome, never travel without at least a cheese sandwich or an apple in your briefcase.

When drinks are offered on trains or airplanes, ask for soda and lime, and sip slowly. One friend of ours carries a package of sunflower seeds with her and nibbles on them one at a time—these have fewer calories than the peanuts usually served, and they're loaded with protein.

If you are an out-of-town speaker, and know that the ubiquitous creamed chicken in patty shells coupled with a chocolate parfait are slated to be served, make the organizer of the event aware of your needs and suggest you'd be delighted with plain sliced chicken, which most hotels and restaurants have on hand all the time. If the dessert is loaded with calories, don't eat it.

Too often women away on business hole up in their hotel rooms and order room service to avoid braving it alone in a restaurant. Why not make the most of your trip? Explore the city's possibilities: Japanese, Chinese, seafood, and vegetarian restaurants are all good bets for the calorie counter. (Thai and Vietnamese eateries are also springing up across the country, and this cuisine is often low in calories.)

Avoid anything with a sweet-and-sour, honey garlic sauce and the deep fried, heavily breaded foods. Oriental restaurants are a dieter's safest haven because they offer stir-fried foods, or foods cooked in soy sauce. A low-calorie dinner at a Japanese restaurant would include sonamoto (a cucumber-style salad) and sukiyaki (thinly sliced lean beef, chinese cabbage, mushrooms, tofu, onions, bean sprouts—all cooked in a marvelous soy-based sauce). Just eat a tiny bit of rice and have the fresh mandarin orange dessert. Bread and butter and rich desserts aren't problems: they're never offered.

THE EXECUTIVE MENU

Here's a sample day's eating on our suggested "exec" plan.

LIFE-LONG EATING HABITS

Breakfast	Calories
1 cup (250 mL) oatmeal with	126
½ tsp. (2 mL) brown sugar	8
1 med. banana, sliced	100
½ cup (125 mL) skim milk	43
1 slice whole wheat toast with	120
1 tsp. (5 mL) corn oil margarine	35
½ cup (125 mL) orange juice	61

Snack	
1 cup (250 mL) unsweetened apple juice	121

Lunch	
1 cup (250 mL) Virgin Mary (tomato juice and lemon)	45
tuna salad sandwich made with ¼ cup (60 mL) tuna drained and rinsed, 1 tbsp. (15 mL) mayonnaise, 2 slices whole wheat bread, lettuce, tomato	325
carrot sticks, 2 tbsp. (30 mL) raisins	135
¼ cantaloupe	45
½ cup (125 mL) skim milk	43

Dinner

Stir-fry ¼ cup (60 mL) diced chicken with ½ cup (125 mL) chopped broccoli, ½ cup (125 mL) celery, ⅛ cup (30 mL) sliced almonds in a little vegetable oil. Season to taste.	190
½ cup (125 mL) brown rice	44
Fresh fruit yoghurt, ½ cup (125 mL) plain yoghurt. Add ½ cup (125 mL) fruit in season, 1 tbsp. (15 mL) honey	160
clear tea	0
	1,601

Stretch your foods by toting some munchies to work: carrots, green peppers, celery, turnip sticks, some raw mushrooms, hunks of broccoli, and cauliflower. Keep them ice-cold by filling a margarine tub or other such container with water. Freeze this and pop your veggies and the tub in a smart container (how about a zipped plastic cosmetic case?). Who knows—the rest of the office might follow suit.

Even compulsive eaters can munch all day long. But the catch (you knew it was coming) is that you eat foods that are low in energy and high in nutrients. There are lots of foods that are "free" or unlimited, and you can have these as often as your schedule permits.

We can't emphasize enough the importance of choosing the right kind of foods as well as the right amounts. Too often women are calorie-conscious only, and run the risk of eating an inadequate amount of nutrients. Never eat less than 1,200 calories a day. This is to ensure your nutrient intake. If for some reason you must eat less than that for any length of time (and only under close medical supervision), take a balanced multiple vitamin-mineral tablet each day.

Here's a list of *very* low-calorie foods you can include in your diet:

- bouillon, clear broth, or consommé
- mushrooms, parsley, watercress
- cranberries, cooked without sugar
- unsweetened pickles
- green peppers
- lettuce, celery, cucumbers, radishes

This doesn't mean that you'll never have another bite of pecan pie, sip a strawberry milkshake or a dry martini, or whatever seems to be your caloric downfall in life. Later on, when your weight has stabilized, you can have these again (occasionally, and in very small amounts).

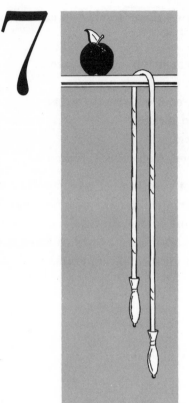

7 Health, Fitness, and the New Woman

Be honest. Are you reading this chapter first? We wouldn't be surprised. Weight control—specifically overweight control—is a multimillion-dollar business and the subject of many best-selling books.

Most of these publications do well because of the widespread belief that life would be far more interesting, that we would become one of the beautiful people, if we could only lose five, ten, or more pounds.

We want to discuss logical (and some illogical) methods of weight control. We also want to emphasize that weight is only one part of total fitness. Other parts of our lives, including food and activity, influence how we cope physically and mentally.

In a search for the perfect food, the elixir of life, exotic eating habits and ideas are often developed. Some people decide to become vegetarians or use health foods or supplements in an attempt to be "superhealthy."

Your health is a precious commodity that can only be maintained — once lost, it's never completely regained. The emphasis in nutrition is prevention — keeping your health, not restoring it after it's been abused. Unfortunately, food or nutrients are not magic. Good nutrition is essential for health, but extra nutrients cannot restore health lost for other reasons.

ARE YOU SURE YOU'RE OVERWEIGHT?

Let's start with a question that most books or weight control programs don't ask: do you really need to try to change your weight?

Why, you ask. Isn't nearly everyone in North America overweight?

That depends on what you call "overweight." There's no clear-cut line between normal weight and overweight. And what may even be normal weight from a health standpoint is considered overweight for the current clingy clothes and Vogue model image. We've become a society obsessed by weight. (And we've got to admit that nutritionists are somewhat to blame.) Yes, there are more overweight people than ever before in North America. And yes, we keep emphasizing that you should get to your ideal weight and stay there. But what is that ideal body weight?

For many years, the standard for body weight was the Metropolitan Life Insurance table of "ideal body weight."

Policy holders with these so-called perfect weights had the lowest death rate.

DESIRABLE RANGE OF WEIGHTS FOR WOMEN

HEIGHT (with 1-in. heels)			WEIGHT (in light-weight indoor clothes)	
ft.	in.	cm	lb.	kg
4	10	147	92-119	42-54
	11	150	94-122	43-55
5	0	152	96-125	44-57
	1	155	99-128	45-58
	2	157	102-131	46-60
	3	160	105-134	48-61
	4	163	108-138	49-63
	5	165	111-142	50-65
	6	168	114-146	52-66
	7	170	118-150	54-68
	8	173	122-154	55-70
	9	175	126-158	57-72
	10	178	130-145	59-75
	11	180	134-168	61-76
6	0	183	138-173	63-79

(Adapted from Metropolitan Life Insurance's *Statistical Bulletin*, Vol. 40, Nov./Dec. 1959.)

Too often these tables became "the bible." And if you were a pound or two over the weight averages, you spent a lot of time and money becoming "ideal" again. It's now believed, however, that a few pounds over the values expressed in the table don't present a significant health risk.

Now's the time to begin to be a little more realistic about weight. Are you really overweight, say thirty pounds or more? Do you have any conditions often found with obesity—high blood pressure, high blood fats, adult-onset diabetes, or gall stones? If the answer to both of these questions is *yes*, then you'll benefit from losing weight. Consult your doctor about counseling by a dietitian or a reputable clinic. And don't move from one fad diet to the next. You'll actually do yourself more harm than good.

Are you a little overweight—even up to ten pounds? You may feel better and think you look better if you get rid of this added weight, but how serious are you about losing? There's no easy way, and it's those last few pounds that don't ever seem to want to disappear. We'll give you some hints, but if you decide it's not worth the effort, then forget the scale and get on with living. There's no point in letting a pound or two of fat dominate your whole life.

Or you may belong to the growing group who are of normal weight but want to weigh even less. This used to be a problem only with women, but more and more men are being caught up in the "thin craze." "Ideal" body size often isn't related to health but to an image—often an unrealistic one. We call it "media-induced paranoia," produced by images continually put before us by the media.

And, finally, there are the truly underweight. (There *are* some, you know.) They get very little attention—except envious looks. And they seldom get any help, although they need it. Life insurance figures show that being underweight can be as serious a health problem as being overweight.

There are two types of underweight people—those who try to gain weight but have difficulty doing so, and those who are underweight because of dieting. The extreme form of this, of course, is anorexia nervosa. Teenagers are most likely to have this life-threatening problem, so we've discussed this fully in Chapter 2. However, more and more women in their twenties are suffering from anorexia.

SPECIAL WEIGHT-LOSS DIETS

There are plenty of these diets. But most of them are very similar. (For example, eighty "new" grapefruit diets appeared in one year.) And many of them are useless, even hazardous.

The grapefruit diet, for instance, claims that grapefruit juice dissolves body fat; that's simply not true. Some of these diets insist on a high number of eggs, adding cholesterol you certainly don't need if you have high blood cholesterol levels or a family history of heart disease.

Fad diets generally *aren't* effective. You may lose some weight at first but you're likely to put it back on ... and then some. Most are irrational and distort or ignore basic principles of biology and nutrition. They promise something for nothing and give magical powers to specific foods or combinations of foods. Fortunately, most are so boring that you're not likely to stay on them too long. But following some of the more extreme, restricted diets for a long time can lead to vitamin deficiencies, anemia, low blood pressure, changes in liver and kidney function, even baldness. Another of our objections is that they don't teach you sound eating habits, eating habits that are necessary for continual weight loss and for keeping the pounds off.

The high-protein, low-carbohydrate diets are perhaps the most popular diets. They include all the "quick weight loss" diets, diet revolutions, and the Scarsdale diet. (This "new" diet was actually introduced in the 1860s.)

There are, in fact, a couple of reasons why cutting down a little on the amount of carbohydrates we eat may be a good idea. First, many high-calorie, sweet foods can be easily eliminated without cutting out a lot of nutrients. And second, by following a diet with a moderate carbohydrate intake, you won't retain as much water while you lose fat, so your weight will drop more quickly. Remember, the huge weight loss some people experience the first few days on the diet is primarily due to water loss.

But severe carbohydrate restriction (to less than eighty grams a day) isn't a good idea. Your blood sugar drops and partially burned fat—called ketone bodies—accumulate in your blood. While you may not feel hungry, no one knows the consequences of this condition. At the very least, it may cause a very bad breath or cause you to faint when you sit up or stand up suddenly.

There are variations of these diets—adding bananas, or using alcohol. (By the way, alcohol gives you seven calories per gram, nearly twice as much as the carbohydrates you're trying to cut out.)

And then there's the other recently popular extreme: the high-carbohydrate, low-fat (and moderate-protein) diet. Its main advocate, Nathan Pritikin, extolls it as part of his overall "plan for longevity." This is one diet that we can support—at least in its general principles and direction, if not in its ultimate goal.

The Pritikin regime, if followed in every detail, would contain only ten to fifteen percent of the calories as fat, and seventy or eighty percent as carbohydrates. This type of diet is typical of many developing countries, and of some oriental diets in our society. It's difficult, however, to get such a low fat intake with the foods available in North America. But more and more low-fat products are becoming available (skim milk cheeses and yoghurts, even reduced-fat meats) as production methods are changed in response to consumers' demands.

So if you want to try the Pritikin diet, go ahead. Remember that all the claims made for the diet have not been proved. And you'll probably not be able to follow the diet completely unless you do all of your own cooking—eating out while maintaining the diet is very difficult. However, a move in the direction of this diet is a sound move towards weight control—and has nutritional and economic advantages as well.

The Beverly Hills diet is very different from most of the currently popular diets, to say the least. It is based on two premises; that anything you can't digest is fattening, that is, it just stays in the body as fat; and that most food is not digestible and must be digested by eating fruits, which are supposed to contain the necessary digestive enzymes. Neither of the above is true. No food can be turned into fat unless it is first digested and absorbed. If it is not digested, it is eliminated from your body in the stool. Also we humans produce our own digestive enzymes in our stomach and intestines so that over ninety percent of all food is digested. The only fruits which contain digestive enzymes are pineapple and green papaya.

The diet is supposedly a "free" one—one that you can tailor to your own likes and needs. However, a very rigid forty-two-day diet plan is spelled out. It starts with pineapple (all you want to eat) and two bananas, and ends with pineapple, papaya, mango, strawberries, or kiwi fruit plus popcorn. With the exception of an occasional fish, pasta or bagel, there's not much variation in between. Many foods, particularily milk products, are eliminated completely. If fact, the diet is lacking calcium, iron, B vitamins, and protein. Even vitamin C may be low because many of the fruits recommended are not the ones really high in this essential nutrient.

You don't need special foods for your weight reduction program. Not only are they expensive, but they may not be what they seem. "Carbohydrate-reduced" does not mean there are no carbohydrates. "Calorie-reduced" in Canada means that the product must have half or less of the calories of the regular product.

Dietetic gum, cookies, candies, ice cream, and fruit spreads are usually sweetened with sorbitol or mannitol; they *do* contain calories. Dietetic chocolate may have extra fat added. Some dietetic fruits are water-packed, but others have a standard amount of sugar.

We suggest you look for some standard low-calorie products—skim milk, dry curd cottage cheese, skim milk cheeses and yoghurt, water-packed, frozen or fresh fruit and light meats. Actually, cutting down fat is a faster way to cut out calories than cutting out carbohydrates. (Fat has nine calories per gram and carbohydrates have only four.)

HOW NOT TO REDUCE

High-protein–low-carbohydrate diets	Includes all sorts of quick weight-loss diets, diet revolutions, and the Air Force diet (which no Air Force will claim). May be high in fat, which is probably not good for your heart. Very low carbohydrate intake may lead to fainting spells.
Banana diets	You may lose weight—not because the bananas are magic but simply because you are not eating much else but bananas. It is, obviously, nutritionally imbalanced.
Grapefruit diets (or Mayo Clinic	The claim that grapefruit dissolves body fat is not true. Some

diet, though no association with the clinic exists)	include a large number of eggs, which are not recommended for those with heart disease.
Liquid or powdered protein diets	A special type of fast (called protein sparing) that was designed to be used only under rigorous medical supervision in a hospital. Results in many adverse side effects including dizziness, nausea, constipation, muscle cramps, dehydration, dry skin, and temporary hair loss. Several deaths have been attributed to improper use of this diet.
Vinegar, lecithin, kelp, and vitamin B$_6$ diets	Includes a balanced 1,000-calorie diet, which will probably result in weight loss. The vinegar, lecithin, kelp, and vitamin B$_6$ are simply unnecessary expenses.

EXERCISE

Fad diets are only one exploitation of the current obsession with weight. Exercise gimmicks and gadgets are enjoying remarkable popularity. Passive exercise, massages, and inflatable suits for spot reduction have been promoted as effortless and quick ways of losing the pounds that took years to accumulate.

Some of these techniques may *appear* to be effective. Sweat and rubberized suits, for example, simply temporarily increase body water loss. And the heat stress that these suits produce may lead to an increased heart rate and higher blood pressure. Dehydration can reduce body weight, and localized pressure can reduce body size by water loss. Unfortunately, both effects are temporary. Weight loss and size reduction quickly return when "rehydration" occurs.

It would be great if there were some magical type of clothing that would aid in weight reduction, either by increasing energy (calorie) expenditure or reducing food intake, or both. But at the moment, the only thing we can recommend is a tight belt or waistband. The resulting discomfort would serve as a reminder that a few pounds could come off your waist (and other places).

Many overweight people really don't eat more than their normal weight counterpart. We can only conclude from this that the major cause of overweight in this country is hypokinesis, or low activity levels. Therefore, exercise becomes an important part of any weight reduction program. But you have to know what exercise can and cannot do.

For example, can you "take inches off the waist, thighs, or buttocks without dieting, with regular exercise in just a few minutes a day," as the magazines claim? Not likely. The energy used for exercise of one specific muscle or set of muscles doesn't come from the fat layer at that muscle. For example, the playing arm (the one most used) of an accomplished tennis player is bigger around than the other arm, but the fat layer is identical for both.

Passive exercise devices that are supposed to do the work for you aren't effective either. The energy expenditure of a group of overweight men was measured while they each had a fifteen-minute massage with a mechanical vibrator. The extra energy used during this period was less than twelve calories. To lose one pound, they would need over 300 treatments. Discouraging, to say the least.

But real exercise, with or without a diet, has three distinct advantages. First, it improves the function of your heart, circulatory system, and muscles. Second, while few people enjoy dieting, exercise and recreational games are enjoyable and may distract you from eating.

Third, the weight lost during exercise is primarily fat; only water and muscle are lost on crash diets. It's believed that hormonal changes that occur during exercise burn up fat and save or conserve lean tissue, which is your ultimate goal. You want to get rid of all those rolls of fat on your tummy, for instance. These same hormonal changes may also decrease appetite.

There's a myth that moderate exercise will increase your appetite. It won't. In fact, vigorous exercise may actually decrease it. Any exercise—walking, climbing stairs—will help burn energy. But for exercise to be effective for fat loss, you should exercise at least twenty to thirty minutes, vigorously enough to use 300 calories per session. A minimum of three sessions a week is required. The amount of energy used each session does not need to be as much if you have four or more exercise periods a week.

Two exercise periods a week, no matter how rigorous the exercise, aren't effective. Neither is very intense exercise for less than about fifteen minutes. Carbohydrates (glycogen), rather than fat, are burned up during these short exercise periods.

WEIGHT CONTROL PROBLEMS

"Fat farms" are profitable ventures. There are so many around that it would be impossible to evaluate them all. However, there are some points you should check before you join any weight control program.

- Is any high-pressure salesmanship involved? Do you have to sign a contract? If so, make sure you are getting your money's worth.

- Is your doctor aware of the fact that you are on a diet? Have you been told by your physician to start a specific program?
- Is there a registered professional dietitian providing the diet outline, recipes, and counseling, or is one available as a consultant?
- Have your present eating habits and nutrient requirements been assessed?
- Are your likes, dislikes, activity patterns, and life style considered when your diet is planned? For example, are you taught how to choose foods wisely when eating away from home?
- Is the diet well balanced nutritionally (have the four basic food groups been included each day: breads and cereals; fruit and vegetables; meat and alternatives; milk and milk products), providing minimum daily nutrient requirements for health, and at the same time allowing for weight loss? A diet of less than 1,000 calories is often nutritionally inadequate, should be followed only under a doctor's and/or dietitian's supervision, and should include a basic multivitamin-mineral supplement.
- Is there an attempt made to change bad eating habits so that weight loss can be maintained on a long-term basis?
- Is there a reasonable rate of weight loss (up to two pounds) per week?

- Are special requirements, such as special foods to ensure the diet's effectiveness, treatments such as hormone shots, involved in the diet? *No research to date has proved the necessity of such treatments.*

Numerous reputable self-help weight management organizations (both commercial and noncommercial) are available. Most offer very good programs that include behavior modification and exercise components as well as realistic diets that basically cover all four food groups. There are even weight control programs offered for adolescents.

The most widely known noncommercial organizations include TOPS, Calorie Counters, and Overeaters Anonymous. Weight-Watchers International, Counterweight, and Diet Workshop are commercial organizations, but are recognized leaders in the weight management field. Contact your local dietetic association or local health unit nutritionist for names of approved nutrition counselors and information on other weight management groups. Another alternative is to ask your physician to refer you to a hospital out-patient dietitian or a dietitian in private practice.

YOUR PERSONAL WEIGHT LOSS PLAN

While there are definitely some very bad weight reduction diets, there is absolutely no single diet good for everybody. Weight reduction is a very individual matter.

If you really need to lose a lot of weight, we recommend that you get professional help, that you join one of the reputable weight control groups, or that you see an out-patient or private practice dietitian. But you may want to lose only a few pounds, or you may not have this type of help available. We'll give you at least some basic guidelines that will help you develop your own specific plan.

First, keep a complete weekly record of everything you eat—what, how much, when, and where you ate it, who you were with, and how you felt at the time.

Next, evaluate what and how much food you ate, according to the COCDS system—*Cut Out, Cut Down, Substitute.* Were there foods that supply mostly calories and nothing else? Foods like sugar and candies can be totally eliminated. Maybe you don't indulge too much in these "caution foods," but you still overeat. In this case, the strategy is to *cut down.* Control the number and size of servings. Then try a little *substituting*: skim milk and skim milk products for whole milk, fresh fruit or skim milk cheese for pies and other high-calorie desserts, soda water for soft drinks.

Look at your food intake record. Are there times, places, and situations that cause you to eat more than you know you should? Parties and visiting with friends may be the downfall of some people, whereas being alone, tired, or bored may cause others to overeat. Identify your own particular weakness.

Energy (calorie) intake, of course, is only one side of the equation. Energy *use* is the other. While you're keeping your record, also record your activity (or lack of it). Only include active sports such as walking or running. You may find that a moderate increase in your activity will improve the weight loss as well as increasing general fitness. Even an hour of daily walking counts.

Finally, list ten changes you want to make in your eating habits, and ten changes you want to make in your physical activity. Be specific: "I'm going to eat less and exercise more" doesn't count. Instead, tell yourself, "I'll walk up the three flights of stairs to work instead of taking the elevator," or "I'll use lemon juice rather than oil dressing on salads."

Now start doing the things you have listed, but only *one at a time*. The idea is to practice each change until it's a habit, then go on to the next, and so on. In time, these new habits will help you not only to shed the weight, but to keep it off once and for all.

COMPULSIVE EATING

Most of us indulge in overeating at least occasionally. But when it happens often and you can't seem to stop, there's cause for concern.

The "binge" eating syndrome, or *bulimia*, is mainly a problem of women in their twenties or thirties. Often, these "sneaky eaters" are well-educated, successful women with emotional problems. Their binges are impulsive and unpredictable and seem to be triggered by stress and self-condemnation. Huge amounts of food are eaten in a short time until finally stomach pain ends the session. The "binger" may force herself to vomit, and more guilt and self-contempt follow.

Women with this condition may or may not have had a previous weight problem. A few have had anorexia nervosa. Some true anorexics do indulge in binge eating occasionally, but the two conditions are different. The typical anorexic is an upper middle-class teenager. Her very low body weight causes menstruation to stop. She is not aware of her problem and does not seek or even want help.

On the other hand, women with bulimia *are* aware of their problem. They do not lose a lot of weight between binges and their menstruation is not affected by their erratic eating habits. Some have a history of drug abuse—

particularly alcohol, barbituates, and amphetamines.

Although there have been no fatal cases, bulimia does damage the stomach and intestinal tract. The constant vomiting and use of laxatives also upset the body's mineral balance. Anyone with these symptoms needs professional help before serious damage is done.

UNDERWEIGHT

Have you ever seen a book on how to gain weight? Well, we haven't either. This topic has long been neglected. Why? Because people who are underweight are in the minority, because the health risk of being underweight is not fully appreciated, and, perhaps most significantly, because the underweight image has become the desirable one in our society.

Just as some people are normally somewhat above the "ideal" body weight, others are normally slightly below it. However, if your weight is twenty percent or more below average, you do have a health problem. You should make an effort to gain some weight and certainly not lose any more.

Eating Strategy   *Weight Gain*

We know that you find it as hard to gain weight as other people do to lose it. The only advice we can give you is to read the earlier section in this chapter, "Your Personal Weight-Loss Plan"—and reverse it. Keep a record to determine what you *don't* eat and why, or why you over-exercise, and when. Then try an "AIAUS" plan, to Add In, Add Up, and Substitute. You can afford more of the "caution" foods if your basic diet is good, or you can just eat more of the nutritious foods. Substitute rich milkshakes for skim milk, or starch (vegetables such as corn or potatoes) for lettuce salads.

SPORTS

Women are moving into many fields once closed to them. One of the last to feel the full impact of women's efforts is the once male-dominated field of Olympic sports, both national and international competitions. Even more encouraging is the fact that girls, teens, and grown women are participating in local, less competitive sports.

But as women enter the sports field, they find all sorts of strange nutrition and food beliefs and practices. We've all heard that athletes need more protein or special vitamins, or that they have a miracle-working pregame meal. This may help, but the benefit is purely psychological. The only thing that athletes need more of than nonathletes is energy.

The energy needed for heavy exercise varies from six to ten calories per minute for women. An hour of exercise, therefore, requires 360 to 600 calories—in addition to your regular energy needs. How well you will perform depends on such innate capabilities as build, muscle structure and biochemistry, on training—and nutrition. Nutrition requires a well-balanced diet.

Only one type of somewhat abnormal diet appears to be of any benefit in competition: the glycogen-loading diet. This "loading" is only beneficial when the event lasts long enough (over thirty minutes) to really begin to draw on the muscles' glycogen stores. If you compete in sports, you may find this diet useful.

The system consists of three phases. In Phase I, the glycogen stores of the muscles are mostly used up by exhaustive exercise of the type to be used in competition. This should be done six to seven days before the event. During a three-day exercise period the diet should be high in fat and high in protein. That means low in carbohydrates, but not *no* carbohydrates. At least 100 g a day should be eaten to prevent the breakdown of body fat which would lead to fatigue and irritability.

In Phase II, a high-carbohydrate diet (250-525 g per day) is followed. This carbohydrate should be from breads, cereals, fruits, and vegetables, rather than from high-sugar foods, to ensure an adequate supply of minerals and vitamins. No exercise is done during this time.

On the day of the event, Phase III, anything goes, as long as the food is eaten four to six hours before the event. (The stomach and upper intestine need to be empty during the event itself.) If the event is a long competition such as a long distance race, diluted sugar solutions can be used for energy. Concentrated solutions can cause stomach cramps.

A note of caution: anyone with cardiovascular disease, diabetes or high serum triglycerides should consult a doctor before trying such a diet. Even those who have none of these conditions should use this only for endurance events and at most two to three times a year before big events.

VEGETARIAN DIETS

Vegetarian eating is becoming more attractive to many people, sometimes for economic reasons, often because of its legendary benefits to health. A vegetarian diet can be nutritionally sound—but it takes some planning and serious thought.

First, what type of vegetarian do you plan to be? If you simply want to avoid red meat and be a "semi" or partial vegetarian, simply substitute poultry, fish, milk, or eggs for meat. You may even cut down the total amount of protein foods you eat each day. Most North Americans get about twice the amount of protein they need. Two servings a day plus your daily two to three glasses of milk should be enough.

If you go one step further and cut out all meats, you'll become a "lacto-ovo" (milk and eggs) vegetarian. This type of diet is fine for any healthy adult or child. Both milk and eggs provide good quality protein plus B vitamins and minerals. But there are a few potential problems. If you are lactose-intolerant (cannot digest the sugar lactose in milk), you'll have to use cheese or fermented milk products. (There is also an enzyme product available that you can use to predigest the milk.) And relying on a large number of eggs is not a good idea if you have high blood cholesterol levels.

But eliminating eggs completely to become a "lacto-vegetarian" may not be wise. Eggs are a fair source of iron, while milk contains almost no iron. Beans, peas, whole grain and enriched cereals, prunes, and molasses also contain iron, but it is not as well absorbed. Along with these, eat foods that are high in vitamin C to increase the absorption of iron.

Total vegetarians, or "vegans," avoid all animal food. Some may restrict their diet even further and eat mainly fruit or raw food. The fewer types of food in a diet, the more difficult it is to get all the nutrients that you need each day.

In our society we think of meat, milk, and eggs as being good sources of protein. We often forget that protein is also found in plant foods, especially beans, peas, cereals, and nuts. But the amount and quality of protein in plant foods is usually lower than that in animal foods. The exception, of course, is soy protein. Soy products such as cakes and soy milk are excellent sources of protein.

You can increase the quality of plant or vegetable proteins by using them in combination with each other or with eggs or milk, if you use these. For strictly plant combinations, the basic rule is to use a grain with a legume (beans or peas). But what about the other essential nutrients contained in the foods that are eliminated in the diet? Can they be supplied by plant foods? Yes, but it isn't easy, and it does take serious planning.

Plant foods are generally rich in vitamins and minerals. There are, however, five nutrients that may not be present in adequate amounts in a strict vegetarian diet: vitamin B_{12}, vitamin D, calcium, iron, and zinc. There are no practical plant sources of vitamins B_{12} and D. Vitamin B_{12} can be obtained from small quantities of milk or egg, fortified soy milk, or soy protein "meat" products. Seaweed or fermented soy are sometimes used as a source of vitamin B_{12}, but no one knows how much of the vitamin they really contain, so you shouldn't rely on them. A good source of B_{12} is nutritional, or food yeast. This contains more B_{12} than other yeasts (Brewer's, Baker's or *liver*) because it is grown in a solution containing much of this vitamin.

Adult vegetarians rarely show clinical symptoms of vitamin B_{12} deficiency. The small quantities they get seem to be adequate. Also, our bodies can store enough B_{12} for several years. But infants don't fare as well. Recently, an infant was found to have a severe B_{12} deficiency; his only food had been breast milk from his vegan mother.

Vitamin D can, of course, be produced in skin exposed to sunlight, and the amounts supplied this way may be enough for an adult—but not for a growing child, especially in areas with long, sometimes sunless, winters. Several cases of rickets in breast-fed babies of pure vegetarian mothers have been reported. The simple solution would be to give recommended amounts of vitamin D supplements to the mother or child. Some soy milks are vitamin D-fortified and should be used for growing children.

Milk is the major source of calcium in the North American diet. The best replacement for regular milk in a strict vegetarian diet is fortified soy milk, which supplies both calcium and vitamin D. Regular, large servings of dark green vegetables (except chard, spinach, and beet greens, in which the calcium is tightly bound to oxalic acid), legumes, almonds or sesame seeds may supply enough calcium for adults—but again, not for growing children.

Iron in plant foods isn't easily absorbed (this can be partly overcome by using a food with a good vitamin C content at each meal). Zinc in plant foods, particularly cereals, isn't used by the body because it is bound tightly to phytic acid. But some of this zinc is released during the yeast fermentation (rising) of bread, so bread should be a part of the diet.

A pure vegetarian diet must be very carefully planned for infants and children. According to one study, heights and weights of strictly vegetarian preschoolers are below the national averages. Cases of *kwashiorkor* (protein deficiency) have also been found in children on these diets.

Adults, on the other hand, may benefit from a partial or total vegetarian diet. Vegetarians tend to be leaner than their nonvegetarian counterparts. They also usually have lower blood cholesterol levels. They may be less likely to develop osteoporosis (bone loss), but this is still debatable.

The vegetarian diet is also low in fat and cholesterol, high in fiber, and usually does not contain many "caution" foods (high in calories, low in nutrients).

HYPOGLYCEMIA

At times we all feel tired and depressed, get hungry, have headaches, and generally don't think as clearly as we should. If you mention this to someone, you may be told that you have hypoglycemia.

Hypoglycemia is now a very popular and socially accepted disorder—just the thing to discuss at cocktail parties. It's an easy way to explain various vague spells of "unwellness" that we all get from time to time. Hypoglycemia literally means low sugar (glucose) in the blood. By low we mean less than forty milligrams per 100 mL. Normally we function with our blood sugar at sixty to 140 mg per 100 mL. Hypoglycemia can cause anxiety, trembling, sweating, fast heart rate, confusion, fatigue, and ultimately unconsciousness. But all of these symptoms can be caused by a number of other things besides the level of your blood sugar.

A lot of people develop hypoglycemia perodically. For instance, if you don't eat for several hours, then eat something that's mainly sugar and do some strenuous exercises, you'll likely develop some of these symptoms.

Another way some people develop hypoglycemia is by drinking distilled alcohol while on a very low-calorie, low-carbohydrate diet. Metabolizing the alcohol in the liver interferes with the formation of glucose, which is necessary to keep the blood glucose up on low-calorie diets. Even if you become weak and dizzy under these conditions, you may not have true hypoglycemia. People who *do* have this condition develop the symptoms a few hours after they have eaten and without doing any strenuous exercise, and this happens frequently.

No one knows how many North Americans actually have hypoglycemia, but it's probably a lot less than the number who think they do. Doctors are reluctant to diagnose this condition because it's overly self-diagnosed. If you have these symptoms, however, and they are a continuing problem, you need a thorough examination, including a five-hour glucose tolerance test. The condition is really pinpointed from the results of a blood test taken while you're experiencing the symptoms.

Ironically, most true hypoglycemia is caused by too much sugar in the diet—not too little. When we eat starches and sugar, our blood glucose rises. Then the pancreas produces insulin to move the blood sugar into the liver and other tissues where it can be used for energy, synthesis of fat, and other functions. In the person with hypoglycemia, the pancreas over-reacts and too much insulin is produced at the wrong time. Too much sugar is moved out of the blood and hypoglycemia results. The body reacts by producing another hormone, epinephrine, in an effort to produce more glucose. Epinephrine is responsible for many of the symptoms of hypoglycemia. The faster the blood sugar level drops, the more likely the symptoms will occur. In fact, if blood sugar drops very slowly, as with long-term fasting, it may reach five to ten milligrams per 100 mL without causing any adverse symptoms.

Contrary to some popular literature on the subject, extra vitamins, special herbs, or supplements will not cure hypoglycemia. In fact, it can't be cured.* But it can be controlled fairly easily. And it should be. The symptoms themselves are a nuisance. Persistent hypoglycemia may

---

* Rare cases due to pancreatic tumors can be cured by removing the pancreas, but the person becomes diabetic.

also indicate early stages of diabetes, especially in obese people.

 Eating Strategy   *Hypoglycemia*

Spread your total food intake over five or six smaller meals each day. Include some protein in each of these meals, as protein is converted to glucose in the liver when it is needed. Also, protein does not stimulate insulin release in the same way glucose does.

Watch the amount of refined or natural sugars you consume. Simple carbohydrates found in sugar, honey, syrups, and even sweet fruit such as oranges, are absorbed quickly after they are eaten. They cause the blood sugar to rise rapidly, which in turn stimulates insulin release. Concentrate on starches from bread, cereals, fruits, and vegetables. These are converted to sugar by digestion, and so are absorbed more slowly than sugars in food.

Alcohol may have to be omitted or limited to one drink a day, depending on your reaction to it. If you drink alcohol, have it with meals, not when you're very hungry.

HEALTH FOODS

It's hard to discuss something you can't define. And that's the situation with health foods. Attempts have been made to arrive at a legal definition. It has been argued, however, that no food should be called "health food," because that would imply that all other foods are "unhealthy foods." This, of course, is not the case at all.

What health foods are depends on what people think they are. We might think of them as good basic foods — salads, yoghurt, whole wheat breads and muffins, fresh fruits. In the supermarket "natural" may mean an absence of artificial colors or flavors in one product, while in another product it may mean that no preservatives have been added.

Historically, natural or health foods generally were limited to foods grown without pesticides and prepared without refining or additives. Such foods are often called organic foods. Unfortunately, this term is also incorrect, as all foods are organic. Milk, for instance, contains ninety-five organic chemicals, and potatoes 150.

Organically grown would be a little closer to the truth; that is, organic fertilizers are used to grow them. But plants take only inorganic compounds (minerals) from the soil. They produce all the organic compounds from carbon dioxide, ammonia, and water. As long as plants get enough minerals from the soil, one source serves as well as any other. It takes a long time, though, for organic fertilizers to decay and to release minerals.

On the positive side, organic materials do tend to improve the consistency of the soil, making it retain water better. So if you want to prepare compost for your garden, it's a great way to recycle kitchen waste, leaves, or grass clippings. But it will not improve either the nutrient values or the taste of the fruits and vegetables you produce.

In some states, there are legal definitions for "organic foods." These may allow a certain amount of pesticide residue. That's a practical decision, as "organic foods" often have been found to have as large an amount of pesticides in them as do regular foods.

The major regulation of health or organic foods is not related to their sale, but to the claims that can be made about them. The use of such terms as "natural," "pure," or "no chemicals added" is forbidden unless these claims can be proved. Dealers often circumvent this restriction by offering information about the product, not on the label, but on sheets that are available when you buy the product.

There's no limitation to the claims that have been made by manufacturers of these foods—herb teas supposed to combat infections, bone meal to lessen anxiety, kelp to cure breast cancer. The inaccuracy of these claims can be dangerous. Health foods and/or supplements are used to treat a variety of medical conditions. They *appear* to work for minor problems (which usually disappear even without treatment). However, more serious conditions may worsen if there is a delay in seeking proper medical help.

Health food stores usually carry more supplements than food. Some of these may be basic multivitamin and mineral preparations, which, in a few instances mentioned throughout this book, may be used for good reason. They may, however, be more exotic, containing such things as kelp, lecithin, choline, bioflavinoids, inositol, and para-amino benzoic acid, none of which are necessary in human nutrition. Of course, you pay a good price for these.

In addition, very high doses of vitamins may be promoted. We've discussed the potential problems of using these in Chapter 8.

"Natural" rather than "synthetic" vitamins are encouraged, again, at a higher price. The body needs special chemical compounds called vitamins, but it doesn't care where they come from. Vitamin C is ascorbic acid, whether it's synthesized from glucose or extracted from rosehips. Some rosehip vitamin C has been found to be "fortified" with synthesized vitamin C.

Two so-called vitamins deserve special mention: "vitamin B_{15}" (pangamic acid) and "vitamin B_{17}," better known as laetrile. Products marketed as vitamin B_{15} are actually varying mixtures of several substances—esters and salts of glucuronic acid, dimethyglycine, glycine (an amino acid), di-isopropylamine, or dichloroacetate, and calcium chloride. None of these has any function as a vitamin. The term "vitamin B_{15}" is a *trade name*.

Because pangamic acid cannot be defined, it is considered a nonexistent substance in the United States and cannot legally be sold. In Canada, pangamic acid can be sold, but no claims of its supposed benefits may be made, either on the bottle or in advertising. This substance has been promoted as a cure for everything from heart disease, nerve and gland disorders, alcoholism, asthma, high blood cholesterol, emphysema, headaches, insomnia, poor circulation, premature aging, rheumatism, and even shortness of breath. But there simply isn't any proof that it is beneficial in the treatment of any of these conditions.

Some of the materials in pangamic acid may also be harmful. Di-isopropylamine acted as a mild sedative and increased blood uric acid levels when it was given to a group of diabetics. One man taking dichloroacetate developed nerve abnormalities; calcium chloride is a well-known poison. In addition, dimethylglycine reacts with nitrites to form two nitrosamines (which produce cancer in animals, although this has not been proved in humans).

Vitamin B_{17}, or laetrile, is another controversial nonvitamin. As one report nicely put it, "vitamin B_{17} contains one or two parts of the sugar glucose, one part benzaldehyde (a mild poison), one part cyanide (a very potent poison) and no parts vitamin." "Vitamin B_{17}," again, is a trade name. It's probably fortunate that laetrile cannot be sold or promoted in the United States or Canada.

Laetrile is a natural poison found in seeds of apples, cherries, pears, apricots and plums, and in nuts such as almonds. It is especially concentrated in the pits of certain types of bitter almonds. (Almond extracts used as flavor-ings have been treated so that they are not poisonous.) Commercial laetrile is taken from apricot pits.

Crushing or chewing apricot pits releases the laetrile. Acid in the stomach, or enzymes found in the plant foods (especially the pits themselves), or in our own cells, release cyanide from the laetrile. The release of the cyanide is speeded up if you are on a vegetarian diet or are taking large doses of vitamin C. Twenty-five to thirty-five apricot pits, or one gram of laetrile, contain fifty to sixty milligrams of cyanide, which is the average fatal dose for an adult.

Cyanide poisoning due to laetrile has killed a number of infants and children. Many more people suffer nonfatal cyanide poisoning. Some of the symptoms of acute poisoning are headache, dizziness, nausea, difficulty in breathing, convulsions, and coma. Chronic poisoning results in muscle weakness and nerve degeneration.

According to its believers, laetrile can cure cancer by releasing cyanide only in the cancer cells. The truth is that more cyanide is released in the healthy cells than in the cancerous ones. In the twenty-five years that laetrile has been promoted as a cure for cancer, not a single successful case has been scientifically documented.

FOOD ADDITIVES

The long list of chemical names that appears on packages scares a lot of people. We tend to fear "chemicals" and admire what we think to be natural. As a result, you may be thinking about cutting back on food additives. That's your choice. But we believe that it should be an educated choice, rather than one based on fear.

Remember, all foods are chemicals. Don't fall for the "natural versus processed" scare. And practically every food contains some natural toxicant. If we applied to all foods the safety standards that are applied to food additives, we would have nothing left to eat. And curiously enough, our own expectations have contributed to the variety of food additives today.

Additives may be used to maintain the nutritional quality of food. For example, some nutrients break down if they're not protected. Vitamin A added to margarine is protected by antioxidants such as butylated hydroxyanisole (BHA), so that you will be sure to get all of this important vitamin.

Additives also are used to preserve the food, so that it may be transported long distances and stored safely; molds, yeast, or bacteria would otherwise make it unfit to eat. Breads and crackers would have to be refrigerated to keep them fresh for more than a few days. Benzoic acid, BHA, BHT (butylated hydroxytoluene), calcium sorbate, citric acid, and vitamin C and its products (ascorbyl palmitate, ascorbyl stearate, or calcium ascorbate) are some of the preservatives now being used for this purpose.

No matter how concerned we are about nutrition and health, our first reaction to any food is to its appearance, then its smell, texture, or taste. So food additives may be used to make food attractive. But legally this cannot be done in a deceptive way; for example, by adding sulfur dioxide to make old meat look fresh.

Would you buy brown strawberry jam or white strawberry ice cream? Probably not, but because we expect certain colors, food coloring has to be added. Many of you may remember working yellow color into margarine, which is naturally white. (Incidentally, one of the colorings in margarines is carotene, a form of Vitamin A.)

Would you want salt to become a solid mass in damp weather because an anticaking agent such as calcium silicate hadn't been added? What about peanut butter or mayonnaise that's oily on top and solid on the bottom because there was no emulsifier such as lecithin or diglyceride? There's a trade-off for everything. And we have to consider just what we'd be giving up if food were additive-free.

Food additives help in food processing and permit large-scale production of foods of constant composition and quality year-round. Some of these additives are used the same way we use them at home. For example, oils (called releasing agents) are used in pans so that baked goods come out without sticking or crumbling. We grease cake pans for the same reason.

The use of food additives for these purposes is strictly controlled by food and drug regulations that specify what additives can be used in what foods and in what amounts. It's not necessary to read these regulations; just read the label of the product you're buying. All of the ingredients added to that food are listed in the descending order of the amount in the food. That is, the first item will be the major part of the food, and the last one will be present in the smallest amount. But if basic ingredients such as flour, margarine, and oils are listed, the additives they contain will not be listed.

Additives wind up at the end of the list because tiny amounts are needed. These amounts vary from less than one percent to a few parts per million or even parts per billion. One part per million is equal to a single drop of vermouth in eighty bottles of gin. A very dry martini, indeed! One part per billion would equal one drop per 500 barrels of gin.

Eating Strategy   *Food Additives*

It is obvious that we don't think it's necessary to be fanatic about avoiding additives. In fact, it's next to impossible to avoid them completely, unless you grow and prepare all of your own food, and that's becoming more and more unlikely in our fast-paced society.

There are some nutritionally sound eating patterns, however, that tend to reduce the amount of additives you'll be getting. These include using fresh produce and meat when they're available and reasonably priced. If you have time, do more cooking "from scratch" and use fewer mixes. Also, all the super high-calorie, low-nutrient foods can be generally eliminated.

8  Looking at Drugs

"Shocking," thought Anne, as she glanced over the morning headlines. "Teenagers Hospitalized for Drug Abuse," "Police Make Big Breakthrough in Heroin Smuggling Ring," "Housewives Becoming Addicted to Tranquilizers."

"Really, what is the world coming to?" But she didn't have any more time to think about that. She finished her second cup of coffee and lit a cigarette (only the third one so far today—it was 8:30 a.m. already). She had to get everything ready for tonight's dinner party. Did they have enough wine and liquor in the house, or would she have to go shopping?

183

She felt a headache coming on—better take an aspirin. And don't forget the vitamin supplement. She was going to need all the pep she could get today.

Your response to the headlines would probably match this woman's. You're glad that you don't take drugs. But don't you? Before you skip this chapter, ask yourself the following questions:

- How many cups of coffee or tea have you had today?
- How many cigarettes have you smoked?
- Have you had a glass of wine, a bottle of beer, or a cocktail?
- Did you swallow a vitamin pill, an aspirin, or an antacid?
- How about the Pill?

If you've answered "yes" to any of these questions, this chapter is indeed for you, as all of these items fit into a drug category—whether it's a social drug (alcohol, caffeine), an over-the-counter drug (aspirin or laxatives), or prescription drug.

Drugs are taken for various reasons. Some are prescribed and may be necessary for health. Others are taken because of habit (coffee) or addiction (cigarettes and hard drugs). But one thing is true of all drugs: they all have side effects. Sometimes these are minor, such as feeling a little jittery if the caffeine in your blood gets too high. Others are major—alcoholism and lung cancer. The side effects we're particularly interested in are those that affect how you get and use nutrients.

The study of food-drug interactions is a relatively new field, but its origins are ancient. Our primitive ancestors discovered through trial and error which plants and animals could be used for food and which would help treat headaches, vomiting, pain, and other problems. Today, most drugs are synthesized rather than being isolated from natural materials. These drugs are more effective and usually have fewer side effects. This has made us forget, however, that nutrition and pharmacology (the study of drugs) have a lot in common.

Drugs are chemicals. Foods are also made up of chemicals. It's not unreasonable that at some point they will come into conflict. But don't panic. Obviously, everyone who takes drugs of any type doesn't immediately develop malnutrition. But you should be concerned if you must use drugs for chronic conditions, if you've smoked for many years, if your coffee cup appears bottomless, or if you drink more than two or three glasses of alcoholic beverages a day. You're also at risk if you're under some stress (just had an operation, for instance) or if you've abused drugs—taken too many, too long. And a poor diet to start with also increases your chances of malnutrition.

There are hundreds of drugs presently in use, but we'll only discuss the ones that many women may use for long periods of time.

SOCIAL DRUGS

Over the past few decades, many women have come to accept the concept of chemical relief to ease the stress and strain of a changed life style.

Alcohol is one way some women relieve the day-to-day stress. And the number of women who smoke continues to climb (in spite of the United States Surgeon General's Report on Smoking and Health).

These comforts are so readily available that we do not

sometimes recognize that we are in fact using drugs. And all of these drugs affect the use of nutrients in some way.

ALCOHOL

As more women enter the executive suite, try to balance a home life with an office life, cope with children (often as a single parent), entertain or travel on business — more and more reach for a tension smoother, often the bottle. But alcohol is two-faced. Sure, it can ease tension and help you slip through social situations. But it can disrupt family life and endanger health. It is both a drug and a nutrient (not an essential one, of course). Paradoxically, it can make you fat or very thin.

Alcohol's effects on health are sometimes contradictory. Studies have shown that nondrinkers or heavy drinkers are more likely to have heart attacks than those who have a couple of drinks a day. One study found that moderate drinkers have high levels of a particular fat in their blood that may protect them from cardiovascular disease.

Before you use this as an excuse to start drinking more, however, remember that alcohol also stimulates the synthesis of fat in your body. And in people with a particular genetic condition in which blood fats called triglycerides are very high, alcohol increases the risk of cardiovascular disease.

Alcohol affects the action of other drugs, either increasing or decreasing their effect. It can also seriously damage the growing infant during pregnancy. Alcohol can damage the heart cells, lead to liver damage (cirrhosis), possibly contribute to cancer of the liver and esophagus, and always decreases the absorption of several essential nutrients.

The difference between the seemingly good side of alcohol and its very definite bad side is the amount you use and the situation in which you use it. For example, alcohol is classed as a nutrient because it supplies energy (about seven calories per gram). On average, an alarming ten to twenty percent of our total calories come from alcohol. These extra calories, added to a normal diet, contribute to the growing amount of obesity and its attendant problems. Even a few drinks a day add up in terms of calories (see the table on page 146 for the calorie value of some drinks).

On the other side of the coin, some heavy drinkers are very thin. This generally happens when alcohol becomes the main item in the diet. Heavy drinkers often don't feel like eating or simply forget to eat. Also, there's evidence that the calories from alcohol aren't used efficiently in the body. Most of the energy from alcohol is used for heat and can't be used for tissue development and repair.

The calories in alcohol are also "empty," that is, alcohol and most alcoholic drinks don't contain protein, vitamins, or minerals. For many years, most of the serious problems of alcoholism were thought to be due to malnutrition. While malnutrition may be a problem, alcohol is definitely a toxic drug. It damages the liver, the bone marrow, the pancreas, and the lining of the gastrointestinal tract.

The damage alcohol causes to the gastrointestinal tract decreases the absorption of thiamin, folic acid, and vitamin B_{12}. Thiamin is also needed in increased amounts so that alcohol will be metabolized by our bodies. And alcohol increases the excretion of magnesium and zinc in the urine. If the intake of any of these nutrients is low, malnutrition may be the result.

Eating Strategy   *Alcohol*

If you drink more than a glass of wine or enjoy several drinks before dinner, keep an eye on your diet. Watch the calories from alcohol (they *do* count). Get plenty of green leafy vegetables, fruit, protein foods, breads, and cereals. The more serious problems—alcoholism and the malnutrition often associated with it—both require immediate professional attention.

SMOKING

Today women are smoking as much as, if not more than, men. Unfortunately, this trend seems to be strongest among teenage girls, who have the added problem of being one of the most poorly nourished groups in North America. In Canada, an estimated 24,000 people die prematurely due to smoking each year, and women are a growing proportion of that group. According to a recent United States report, the death rate from lung cancer among women in that country has doubled since 1960. If this trend continues, by the year 2000 lung cancer is expected to pass breast cancer as the number one cancer in women.

Obviously the best way to prevent these deaths would be for smokers to quit. However, many either can't or won't, so various ways to decrease the bad effects of smoking are being sought. One interesting study found that smokers who followed a good diet, one particularly high in green leafy vegetables and other foods containing vitamin A, had a lower incidence of cancer than smokers on a poor diet. Vitamin A compounds are also being tested as a means of preventing the recurrence of cancer (in people, for example, who have already had one cancerous lung removed).

Smoking has many other adverse effects on the body, most of which can't yet be explained. Smokers don't use protein efficiently, and they have low blood levels of amino acids, glucose, and fatty acids, all vital to our overall health. Women who smoke develop a more severe form of osteoporosis (loss of bone minerals) than nonsmokers.

Smokers may also have low blood levels of vitamin C. This is because smoking activates an enzyme in the intestine that destroys this essential nutrient before it can be absorbed. The absorption of vitamin B_{12} is also decreased, but the reason for this is not yet known.

From a nutrition standpoint, the most serious effect of smoking is not on the woman, but on her unborn baby. Smokers produce smaller babies and have more premature deliveries, abortions, stillbirths, and neonatal (newborn) deaths than nonsmokers. This is covered in detail in Chapter 3.

Fear of gaining weight is the most common excuse given for not quitting. Research has shown, however, that only one-third of those who stop actually gain weight. Surprisingly, another one-third even lose weight.

Eating Strategy *Smoking*

Smokers need foods high in vitamin C: eat plenty of fresh fruit. Strawberries and green peppers are good sources of vitamin C. Other good vitamin C foods are broccoli, Brussels sprouts, watermelon, citrus fruit, citrus fruit juices, or other juices with added vitamin C. Even cauliflower and liver will help.

CAFFEINE

Caffeine is a little stimulant that goes a long way! Eighty-five percent of those over eighteen have some caffeine each day, according to an American study, and in Ontario some ninety percent of adults use caffeine daily. The average daily intake was found to be 186 mg (about two cups of regular coffee). Some individuals, however, had more than 500 mg a day.

Caffeine and its relationship to heart disease, ulcers, sleep disturbances, bladder cancers, and anxiety has been the subject of many studies. But the association of caffeine to these disorders is very controversial.

Caffeine acts as a mild stimulant to relieve minor fatigue and boredom. It stimulates the heart and central nervous system. It also acts as a diuretic—causes the kidneys to increase urine output. It is a mildly addicting drug. Heavy coffee, tea, or cola drinkers who stop drinking these beverages may experience depression or headaches for a few days.

Headache and cold remedies contain about thirty milligrams of caffeine per tablet. And, of course, "stay awake" pills are really loaded. Chocolate also has some caffeine. Check the following table, a guide to drinks, drugs, and foods containing caffeine.

CAFFEINE CONTENT

ITEM	METHOD	MG/CUP (/250 mL)
Tea[1]	In bag	58 to 65
Tea	Infused in metal ball	58
Tea	Loose	77
Tea	Instant	48-62
Coffee[1]	Ground	85
Espresso	Ground	150
Coffee	Instant	60
Regular cola[2]		18-24

ITEM	MG/CUP
Diet cola	18-21
Cocoa	50
Decaffeinated coffee	0.18-3.3

	MG/TABLET
Headache and cold tablets	30
Stay-awake pills	100
1 chocolate bar (40 g)	20

1. Caffeine in coffee or tea can vary widely depending on the strength of the brew, the size of the cup, and, in the use of coffee, whether it's perked or instant.

2. There are few government restrictions on the use of caffeine. The law does state that soft drinks sold in Canada must not contain more than 200 parts per million or approximately 57 mg/10-oz. (/380 mL).

 Eating Strategy   *Caffeine*

Some people become jittery, can't sleep, or have chest pains when they use caffeine. If you want to cut down:

- Favor tea over coffee, keeping in mind that shorter brewing time produces less caffeine. Or use decaffeinated coffee.
- If you do drink coffee, use an instant, rather than coffee made by "perks" or "drips." Drink more water, fruit juices, and less cola. Try *café au lait* for a change. Limit your intake of foods and beverages containing caffeine. Aim for a count of no more than 200 to 300 mg per day (about three or four cups of coffee). When you take drugs containing caffeine, decrease caffeine from other sources accordingly.

OVER-THE-COUNTER DRUGS

Remember that the major drug-nutrition problems are not due to the use of illicit drugs, but to the misuse of legal ones. The plethora of seemingly innocent over-the-counter drugs such as aspirin, mineral oil, laxatives, and antacids is a hidden nutritional minefield. And vitamins too can be surprisingly dangerous.

It is simply impossible to discuss all the drugs now in use, but we'll deal with some of the more common ones. If you must take any drug for a long time, be sure to ask your doctor about its potential nutritional side effects. There may not be any, but it's better to be sure.

Antacids are among the worst offenders because they interfere with the absorption of phosphorus and thiamin. Long-term use of antacids to treat stomach problems (likely due to overindulgence—too much food or booze) can lead to weak muscles because of the phosphorus depletion, and skin and nerve changes due to thiamin deficiency.

Try to use antacids as little as possible, and make sure you get enough protein foods, whole grain or enriched breads and cereals.

Mineral oil is the favorite laxative of many women, especially older women. But as little as four teaspoons two times a day interferes with absorption of vitamin A, D, E, and carotene (which changes to vitamin A in our body).

You can probably stop taking laxatives altogether if you eat lots of foods containing fiber—whole grain cereals, fruits, and vegetables. If you try this and still have a problem, ask your doctor to suggest a laxative other than mineral oil.

A few other laxatives also have potential ill effects.

Phenolphthalein may lead to phosphate depletion and to bone demineralization. Bulking agents slightly decrease the absorption of fat, protein, and minerals such as iron and zinc. There is generally no problem with these unless your diet is already low in these nutrients.

The old standby, *aspirin* (or its equivalent), is misused by many, although it must be used to treat conditions such as arthritis. Large quantities interfere with the body's protection of the walls of the stomach. This can result in gastrointestinal bleeding, leading to anemia and gastric ulcers. Taking three to nine aspirins daily causes bleeding in seventy percent of people. Aspirin also interferes with the action of vitamin C in the blood.

If you rely heavily on aspirin for medical reasons, try to get the newer, coated pills that do not damage the stomach as much, and eat foods rich in iron (leafy green vegetables and meat, especially organ meats).

VITAMINS AND MINERALS

Perhaps you've never regarded vitamins and minerals as over-the-counter drugs. Large doses of these should be treated as drugs, as they can be just as dangerous, even deadly. Vitamins are being promoted as a cure for practically everything today, even some of the drug effects we have discussed. Therefore, it is especially important to be aware of some of their toxic properties (see the following table). People respond to massive doses of vitamins differently. Some may have no apparent ill effect while others may develop serious symptoms even with lower doses.

The effects of overdoses of fat-soluble vitamins have been known for years. Canada has the dubious distinction of having the first recorded death due to a *vitamin A* overdose. Arctic explorers made the fatal mistake of eating polar bear liver; three ounces contain a lethal dose of vitamin A.

Polar bear liver isn't a common food. Many of us, however, have a lethal dose of vitamin A sitting in a bottle of vitamin pills. Deaths are rare, but you can get headaches, diarrhea, and experience vomiting and hair loss from too much vitamin A. It has been claimed that vitamin A is an effective way to prevent or treat sunburn. In fact, too much of this vitamin will make your skin peel.

POTENTIALLY TOXIC VITAMINS AND MINERALS *

NUTRIENT	TOXICITY
Vitamin A	Long-term (chronic) dose: 20-60,000 I.U./day, children; 100,000 I.U. adults Acute dose: 1,000,000 I.U. Symptoms: Headache, dizziness, irritability, drowsiness, coma, fits, diarrhea, vomiting, hair loss, loss of appetite, joint and muscle pains
Vitamin D	Chronic dose: 2-3,000 I.U./day, infants; 50,000 I.U. adults Acute dose: Unknown Symptoms: High blood calcium levels accompanied by loss of appetite, nausea and weight loss, bone demineralization, headaches, fatigue, and confusion
Vitamin E	Dosage: Unknown Symptoms: Recent studies in humans indicate that large doses of vitamin E may interfere with vitamin K activity and, therefore, with blood clotting

*Due to overdoses.

Vitamin C	Dosage and symptoms not established in humans. Animal studies indicate that massive doses lead to abnormal breakdown and demineralization of bones. Possibility of vitamin C deficiency (see page 196).
Niacin (nicotinic acid, nicotinamide)	Nicotinic acid in large amounts leads to flushing, burning, and itching skin
Folic acid	15 mg per day: Altered sleep patterns, irritability, and overactivity
Iron	Chronic: Iron accumulated in liver (cirrhosis), skin (bronzing), pancreas (diabetes), and heart (heart failure) Acute: Lethargy, vomiting, diarrhea, weak and slow pulse, hypotension, shock
Zinc	Interferes with absorption of iron
Fluoride	Normal fluoridation at 1.0 ppm. has no toxic effects; 4-8 ppm., brown spots on teeth known as fluorosis; 8-20 ppm., overcalcification of ligaments; 50 ppm., growth retardation

Note: Most of these symptoms can result from other causes. But if you are taking large doses of vitamins or minerals and notice any ill effects, stop taking the supplements and consult your doctor.

Vitamin D is a paradox. If you don't get enough, your bones become weak; if you get too much, your bones become weak. Vitamin D is essential for calcium absorption and for depositing this mineral in bones. If too much vitamin D is used, however, the calcium leaves the bones and becomes deposited in soft tissues such as the heart, the kidneys, and the liver. If you drink two to four glasses of vitamin D-fortified milk a day, don't take vitamin D supplements.

Sales of *vitamin E* have almost doubled in the last five years. Men have been most interested in this vitamin because of its reported magical effect on sexual powers or ability to increase athletic performance. However, large doses of this vitamin haven't been successful in treating human sterility or impotence. Studies have also shown that vitamin E doesn't increase the performance of either swimmers or runners.

Women are also gulping vitamin E to try to delay aging or prevent angina pains (neither effect has been proved). It appears that vitamin E, in the amounts now used (400 I.U.), is not nearly as toxic as vitamins A and D. However, it's also a fat-soluble vitamin and can be stored to some degree in the body. A few cases of abnormally slow blood clotting due to large doses have been reported. And in one controlled study, 300 I.U. of vitamin E taken daily for three months led to high levels of blood triglycerides (a type of fat) in women but not in men.

We need only about six to ten milligrams of vitamin E a day. You can get this from common foods such as green leafy vegetables, whole grain cereals, and vegetable oils.

For many years, water soluble vitamins such as *vitamin C* were believed to be completely nontoxic. But that was before we started mega-dosing ourselves. Now the old rule that there are really no nontoxic substances, just nontoxic amounts, is being demonstrated.

Vitamin C, a water-soluble vitamin, has been widely acclaimed as a cure for colds. This effect has not been proved, but several studies, including one at the University of Toronto in 1972, show that moderate amounts (about 250 mg per day) may decrease the length of general winter illness.

Any excess water-soluble vitamins you consume are excreted in your urine. (North Americans have the distinction of producing the most expensive urine in the world!) In the case of vitamin C, that extra excretion causes problems. It makes accurate testing for diabetes difficult because it gives a false indication of urine sugar levels. Vitamin C makes the urine very acidic. This may simply irritate the skin or may cause kidney stones (the uric acid or "cysteine" type). Also, because some people on high doses of vitamin C tend to excrete more of a substance called oxalate than usual, oxalate stones may develop.

For most, the major danger of large doses of vitamin C is discontinuing them. Your body becomes accustomed to excreting large amounts of this vitamin. It keeps on doing this for a while after the supplements are discontinued, and some mild symptoms of scurvy have been reported. So if you decide to reduce the amount of vitamin C you may be taking, do so slowly.

The potential toxicity of the *B vitamins*, which are also water-soluble, hasn't been extensively tested. However, nicotinic acid can cause temporary problems, such as facial flushing. The study of niacin as a means of possibly decreasing cardiovascular disease was stopped because the amount being used (three grams a day) was causing liver damage.

Minerals can also be toxic. The differences between inadequate, adequate, and toxic amounts are even less than for vitamins. The major concern in this area in North America is acute iron overdoses. The reported cases have been children who took too many supplements containing iron. But a greater control of advertising and availability of these products, as well as child-proof bottle tops, has helped solve this problem.

It is difficult for adults to get too much of a vitamin or mineral from just eating food. But it is dangerously easy to get too much through pills. Many people believe that if a little of each vitamin is necessary for normal good health, larger amounts will make them "superhealthy." That's just not true. Yet this belief leads many to waste their money and endanger their health by taking many vitamin pills a day, or taking the mega or high-potency vitamins now sold in the United States. In Canada, the amounts of each vitamin that can be in one pill are strictly controlled. It's the individual who decides whether to take one or fifty pills a day. Large doses of vitamins are useful in treating a few, very rare diseases. At these high doses, the vitamins become drugs, not nutrients, and must be treated as such.

Vitamin and mineral supplements must never be considered a replacement for a balanced diet. They should be used, as the name implies, as supplements only, and only in cases where a good intake of nutrients from foods isn't possible—for instance, with a severely restricted diet caused by illness or food intolerance.

Many multivitamin preparations correspond fairly well to a reasonable intake of vitamins and minerals. Others contain higher doses of the nutrients. These so-called "high-potency" pills are often labeled "For Therapeutic Use Only." Take that label seriously and use only if the pills have been prescribed by your doctor after tests have indicated your need for them.

In our opinion, supplements aren't necessary except

in special cases. But if you've decided you're going to take a supplement, check the label against the values on the table that follows. Also, make sure you are not paying for things you don't need (like garlic and parsley). Buy the least expensive and lowest dosage possible from a reputable manufacturer. Widely advertised and "natural" brands are no better (and are often more costly) than the house brands or synthesized vitamins. And don't forget that vitamins can deteriorate with time. Check the expiry date and store away from direct heat and light.

VITAMIN SUPPLEMENTS*

Thiamin (B_1)	1.0 mg
Niacin (B_2)	14.0 mg or NE
Riboflavin	1.3 mg
Vitamin B_6	1.5 mg
Folate or folic acid	200.0 μg
Vitamin B_{12}	3.0 μg
Vitamin C	30.0 mg
Vitamin A	800 RE or 2,000 I.U.
Vitamin D	2.5 μg or 100 I.U.
Vitamin E	6.0 mg
Calcium	700 mg
Magnesium	250 mg
Iodine	100 μg
Iron	14 mg
Zinc	9 mg

*Based on the Canadian Recommended Daily Nutrient Intake. Larger doses are not necessary and are potentially harmful.

PRESCRIPTION DRUGS

Perhaps you didn't realize you shouldn't swallow a tetracycline pill with a glass of milk. Or that you should avoid aged cheese or Chianti wine if you're taking an antidepressant. If you are taking a drug, the food you eat can cause the drug to act faster, slower, or not at all.

The extent of the interaction between drugs and food depends on the type of drug, the dosage, your age, size, and specific medical condition, as well as the specific type of food.

The effect of a drug can be speeded up or slowed down if there's food in your stomach. This is why your doctor will often tell you to take some drugs with meals and others on an empty stomach. *Tetracycline* (an antibiotic) taken with dairy products is a prime example. The calcium in milk, cheese, and yoghurt slows down the absorption of tetracycline; therefore, you shouldn't take that particular drug with a glass of milk.

But drinking orange or other citrus fruit juices with *iron supplements* is recommended as the acidic juice increases the absorption of iron. Generally, though, fruit juices and carbonated beverages are too acidic for most drugs. They cause the drug to dissolve too quickly in the stomach, where it's hard to absorb, rather than in the intestine, where it is absorbed more easily. If in doubt, use water to swallow drugs unless you have been given other specific instructions.

One of the most hazardous food/drug interactions is between some drugs (called MAO inhibitors) used to treat depression and foods such as aged cheese, Chianti wine, and chicken livers. These drugs prevent the breakdown of natural substances such as tyramine contained in these foods. Excess tyramine in the blood leads to soaring blood pressure, severe headaches, or even brain hemorrhages.

If you are given a drug for depression, ask your doctor what it contains. If it has a MAO inhibitor, avoid foods that contain tyramine, such as pickled herring, salami, pepperoni, sharp cheese, beef and chicken livers, yoghurt and sour cream, beer, most wines, soy sauce, and protein extracts.

Drugs can also affect the way your body uses the vitamins and minerals in foods. *Diuretics* or water pills, for example, increase the loss of potassium in the urine. You should eat foods with a high potassium content, such as oranges and tomatoes and their juices, figs, raisins, bananas, prunes, potatoes, squash, and cantaloupe. Check with your doctor; there are diuretics available that don't cause potassium loss.

CONTRACEPTIVES

Oral contraceptives, more commonly called the Pill, have been taken by so many women for so many years with so many side effects that they need special attention.

While oral contraceptives have an important role to play in controlling the growth of the world's population, they may also present a few nutritional problems for women.

More than fifty metabolic changes have been associated with the use of the Pill. By changing the body's hormone levels, it affects carbohydrate, lipid, protein, mineral, and vitamin metabolism. The positive effect of these changes is that women on the Pill may need less iron because oral contraceptives tend to reduce menstrual blood loss and to increase "iron-binding" capacity (that is, the ability to absorb iron).

But women differ from men in the way in which they "use" or metabolize vitamin C. During certain phases of the normal menstrual cycle, women have higher blood levels of this vitamin. The Pill appears to stop these typical fluctuations of levels of C in the blood, creating a need for a higher intake of vitamin C by Pill users.

Oral contraceptives also interfere with the absorption of the type of folic acid found in food, but not the type usually found in supplements. Therefore, women on the Pill should get abundant amounts of this vitamin, preferably from green leafy vegetables. Young girls are more likely to have folic acid deficiencies—generally because their diets are often already poor. Folic acid deficiency can lead to macrocytic anemia.

The Pill increases thiamin, riboflavin, and vitamin B_{12} requirements slightly. It also increases the absorption of copper and zinc.

The Pill's interference with vitamin B_6 metabolism can mean a deficiency of this important vitamin, leading to a feeling of general depression. Vitamin B_6 supplements have been given to some women on the Pill to relieve this depression—but its widespread use is still controversial.

Side effects of Pill use such as headaches, depression, and nausea, may also be related to your food habits. Report any of these symptoms to your physician.

Even nondrug methods of contraception may alter nutrient needs. For example, the *IUD* can result in heavier and longer menstrual periods. The increased blood loss increases iron needs. If these aren't met, anemia may result. Eating meat, eggs, whole grains, green vegetables, and dried fruit will give you the iron you require.

Eating Strategy   *The Pill*

Usually, careful food selection will meet the needs of pill users. Why not take the Pill with a glass of orange juice—a quick way to get both the vitamin C and the folate at one gulp.

Perhaps you gained weight when you went on the

Pill. Women average about a six-pound (3-kg) weight gain caused by an increase in body fluids. Check your calorie and exercise activity pattern if you've gained more weight than that. Maybe you should be cutting back in your eating a bit—or exercising more. But also ask your doctor, who may recommend a different type of Pill.

Eating Strategy   *Drugs: Summary*

If you're on medication, here's what you can do to prevent some food/drug interactions:

- Follow your doctor's orders about when to take the drug and what foods and beverages to avoid, or which you should emphasize. If you will be on medication for a prolonged period, ask for a referral to a hospital or a private practice dietitian to help modify your diet as needed.
- Eat a well-balanced diet that includes a wide variety of foods. Use of a needed drug is less likely to cause depletion of vitamins and minerals if your overall nutritional status is good.
- Alcohol doesn't mix with a lot of medications. As a rule of thumb, avoid alcohol when you're using drugs of any kind.

In the United States, the FDA is trying to make labeling of over-the-counter drugs more informative. These drugs are being reviewed for safety, effectiveness, and labeling claims. Perhaps manufacturers will have to provide more detailed information on how drugs react with other drugs or with food.

9 The Older Woman

Nutritional requirements, food preferences, and eating habits change throughout our lives. We know a great deal about what's best for infants, what an active teenager should eat, and the special requirements for pregnant women. But special nutritional requirements for the elderly are just beginning to be of interest, for two reasons.

First, the number of older people in the population is the highest it has ever been in our history, and it is steadily increasing. Eight percent of North Americans were sixty-five or older in 1976; by 2030, twenty-five percent will be over sixty-five. The average life expectancy of an American was forty-seven in 1900; today it is seventy-three. Second, many older people are either marginally or completely malnourished. In this instance, women seem to fare somewhat better than men. As a group, older men, particularly those who live alone, are one of the two least well fed groups in our society (the other is teenage girls).

The main nutrition problems of the elderly are over- or underweight, irregularity, bone decalcification (osteoporosis) and some vitamin deficiencies. These problems arise because some of our nutrient needs change as we become older. Also, eating may not be as enjoyable as it once was because of dentures, heartburn, constipation, loss of taste buds — or even loneliness. Low incomes, distance from supermarkets, lack of transportation, a change in eyesight or hearing, cultural preferences — these are all factors that may make it hard to eat properly.

It's often easier to pop a slice of bread (or three or four) in a toaster, slather it with butter and jam, and drink cups and more cups of sugary tea, rather than cook a balanced meal. But remember that sound nutrition habits have never been more important than at this stage, even if they do take a little extra effort.

WEIGHT CONTROL

Being *overweight* is a problem for a great many older people. Forty percent of females and thirty percent of males over sixty-five are overweight. And obesity, as we've pointed out before, is connected to heart disease, hypertension, and diabetes.

The need for food energy declines as we age, and this is why we may start gaining weight after forty. Our basal metabolic rate (the energy required just for living) drops about sixteen percent between the ages of thirty and seventy. This is because our total muscle is decreasing. Also, we may not exercise as much as we get older, so we have to eat less than before.

This "energy balance" may be the most pressing nutritional challenge we must face in later years because it presents a problem: while calories should be reduced, nutrients definitely should not. We still need all the essential nutrients each day.

But how do you get the nutrients without also including the calories? Easy. Choose the right food by following *Canada's Food Guide* or the *Basic Four*, which classify food into the following four groups.

Bread and Cereals supply protein, iron, several B vitamins, and energy. (Remember, it's not the bread that's fattening, it's the quantity you eat—and the extras you add.) And whole grain cereals and bread supply the fiber you need to stay regular. Pick three servings a day from this group: a slice of whole grain bread, a half cup of cooked cereal, pasta, or a muffin. Try fresh fruit in cereals rather than buying the "presweetened" kind.

Fruit and vegetables are important because they can supply the nutrients without a high energy cost. They are good sources of vitamin A (for example, cantaloupe, spinach, broccoli) and vitamin C (for example, citrus fruit, strawberries, tomatoes, watermelon). We need four to five servings from this group. One cup (250 mL) of fresh, canned, or frozen vegetables (or their juice), or one fruit is considered a serving. Try keeping some vegetables to nibble on in the refrigerator—even a marinated vegetable salad that isn't as perishable as fresh vegetables is a good idea. (Keep in mind a plain baked potato has ninety calories, the same potato fried has 185!) Go easy on the butter you add to vegetables. Try lemon juice and other seasonings instead. Buy water-packed canned fruit, if fruit is out of season. And watch those salad dressings!

Milk and milk products are a great source of calcium, and a good calcium intake, along with physical activity, are important in the prevention of osteoporosis (discussed later in this chapter). Milk also supplies other nutrients—protein, riboflavin, and vitamins A and D. Two servings are recommended from this group: a cup (250 mL) of milk, yoghurt or cottage cheese, plus one and one-half ounces (45 g) of hard cheese, for instance. Use skim or 2% milk, and buy plain yoghurt (add your own fresh fruit).

Meat and alternatives are foods rich in protein, needed for repair of cells, body tissues, blood, organs, skin, and hair. Food in this group gives you the iron and the B vitamins you need.

Choose one and a half to two servings from this group each day: about two to three ounces (60 to 90 g) of lean meat, chicken, fish. Or two eggs, a cup (250 mL) of dried peas, beans, or lentils, and a cup (250 mL) of milk would do the trick. If you're on a low-cholesterol diet, use low-fat milk or cheese, nibble on more poultry, fish, and lean meat, and eat a maximum of three eggs a week. Trim all the fat from meat and skin from poultry. And don't fry foods. Try using the natural juices of meat as gravy.

WEIGHT MANAGEMENT

Selecting food from the four groups will supply about 1,200 to 1,500 calories a day. If you're trying to lose weight, pick the lower number of servings from the group and in that group select the food with the fewest calories; spinach instead of corn, cheddar instead of cream cheese, for instance. (You're going to have to forget all those "dangerous delectables" like chocolate eclairs, creamy cheese-cakes, and cream-filled donuts.) Common sense and an inexpensive calorie chart will help. A word of caution. Never attempt to lose more than two pounds a week—more than that is too great a shock to your system. Never go on a diet that is less than 1,200 calories a day.

Watch the hidden calories in the "extras"—the fats, sugar, alcohol, and high-calorie goodies. Sure, you can enjoy an occasional piece of lemon meringue pie... but don't overdo it. High-calorie foods that don't contain many nutrients may dull your appetite for the more nutritious foods you need.

And read the section on weight control in Chapter 7.

Being underweight can be as severe a problem as being overweight. It may simply be the result of not eating enough food. In that case lack of essential nutrients can lead to depression, fatigue, and anemia. If you eat hearty meals but are still quite underweight, see your doctor to check for any digestion or absorption problems.

NUTRIENT DEFICIENCIES

Older people eat about twenty percent less food than younger people, and as a result may obtain fewer essential nutrients. Again, we emphasize that nutrient requirements do *not* decrease with age. One exception is iron. A woman needs less after menopause. But even with that change, iron deficiency still appears to be a problem with five to forty percent of older people—and this deficiency accounts for the anemia that often results.

About one-third of those over sixty-five who are not in institutions suffer deficiencies in vitamin B_{12} and folate. Too few vitamins and minerals seem to account for other symptoms of the elderly such as loss of appetite, fatigue, slow healing, little response to therapy, and confusion.

Popping vitamin pills isn't the answer. Self-medication with massive doses of potentially toxic vitamin and mineral supplements is a dangerous and expensive game. And too often the nutrients that older people take are not those lacking in their diets. Take supplements only if they are prescribed after a thorough checkup.

The best strategy to combat nutrient deficiency is to review the basic foods discussed under weight control and to emphasize the high nutrient foods in your diet.

BONE LOSS (OSTEOPOROSIS)

We're all familiar with cases of elderly women falling and fracturing a hip or an arm. Often, these fractures occur spontaneously; even a simple task like opening a window can cause a fracture in a victim of *osteoporosis* (a process of severe bone deterioration).

Some bone loss is normal. Starting at birth, our bones are constantly being formed, broken down, and then rebuilt. It's a slow, continuous process. Until we reach adulthood, bones form faster than they break down. Then, for some reason, in middle age the bone loss speeds up and outdistances the growth of the new bone. If this continues over a long enough time, we end up with smaller, more fragile bones. Persistent back pain, "shrinking," and the familiar dowager's hump are all signs of this condition. Eventually the loss of height and the bent spine cause pressure on the stomach area, which in turn can lead to digestive problems. This bone loss takes many years and usually cannot be detected in the early stages. Thirty percent of the bone must be lost before it can even be seen on an x-ray.

Women are more susceptible than men to osteoporosis. Changes in hormonal balance at menopause, for example, accelerate bone loss. (Estrogen treatments are sometimes used in the treatment of osteoporosis, but the results haven't been completely successful.)

It is estimated that thirty percent of women over thirty-four in North America suffer from the problem, and that it is the major form of bone loss in elderly women. Yet in other countries of the world, parts of Asia and Africa, for example, osteoporosis is rare. Factors other than aging obviously have an influence, and the goal now is to identify these factors so osteoporosis can be treated, or better still, prevented.

Many possible causes are being examined: heredity, physical activity (or lack of it), hormones, and, of course, diet. Physical activity seems to discourage the development of osteoporosis. And conversely, a low level of activity, particularly in extreme cases (confinement to bed, for example), does increase bone loss.

What about dietary factors? The most obvious culprit seems to be calcium, because it is such an important part of bone structure. However, adding and removing calcium from the bone is influenced by other factors, such as protein. We do need protein to form a base for the calcium salts in the bone. But in North America we eat too much. And a surplus can counteract the positive effects of our calcium intake.

The effects of fluoride are being studied. This mineral combines with calcium-phosphorous salts of the bone to make it more resistant to osteoporosis.

We've pointed out the significance of calcium. Some recent findings have indicated that osteoporosis can be halted or sometimes reversed by diets providing about

1,500 mg of calcium each day. However, a United States survey of more than 5,000 women aged forty-five or over found that the average daily calcium consumption was only 450 mg—forty-five percent below the 800 mg recommended in the United States and Canada.

 Eating Strategy   *Bone Loss*

We can only make a few suggestions based on what is known at the moment:

- Watch your protein intake. Two to three moderate servings of protein food a day are all that is necessary.
- Get a good calcium intake. Fluid milk and nonprocessed cheese are your best sources.
- If you have fluoridated water, you should be getting enough fluoride. If you don't, fluoride supplements shouldn't be taken unless they are prescribed for you. Fluoride in excess amounts can be toxic, even deadly.

If you do suffer from osteoporosis, we can't stress strongly enough that you *check with your doctor* before you begin any dietary program to control this disorder.

CONSTIPATION

Constipation problems seem to increase as we age; therefore fiber becomes more important. Our grandparents used to refer to fiber as roughage. Perhaps we should call it "smoothage," as it really helps our intestines work smoothly.

Fiber is simply an indigestible carbohydrate that gives form to our food. It is plant material that is not used by the body directly as a nutrient. Since fiber isn't broken down by chopping, crushing, or cooking, it stays in our digestive tract and absorbs water. This spongelike action has a laxative effect, helping to cleanse our system, relieve constipation, and regulate elimination.

Over the last fifty years, our consumption of high-fiber foods such as whole grains, fruits, and vegetables, has declined. Instead, we are eating more refined foods—and the effects are noticeable in our overall health. Recent research indicates that a diet low in fiber can lead to various problems. Dr. Denis Burkitt, a leading researcher on fiber, has found a connection between a low-fiber diet and such ailments as cancer of the colon, appendicitis, diverticulitis, constipation, and heart disease.

You don't have to make radical changes in your diet or give up your favorite foods just to get the fiber you need for good digestive functioning. Whole grains, fresh fruits and vegetables, dried peas, dried beans, figs, dates, nuts, and seeds are all good sources of fiber.

How much fiber should you have each day? There simply isn't any recommended intake guideline. The average North American gets about twenty grams of fiber a day. Probably, this should be increased to thirty to forty grams, although people differ in their tolerance of high-fiber foods (particularly beans and peas).

Fiber supplements such as bran tablets are on the market. Each little tablet contains one-quarter gram of fiber. You'd have to gulp about eighty of these pills daily to get the recommended amount! It's easier, and cheaper, to eat a slice or two of whole wheat bread and munch an apple.

Eating Strategy *Fiber*

- Include a wide variety of vegetables and fruits with edible skins, beans, and peas in all your meals.
- Eat whole fruit rather than drinking juices. Use fruit instead of sugar to sweeten cereals.
- Sprinkle wheat bran or a bran cereal on other cold or cooked cereals.
- Use whole wheat flour when you bake and be sure not to sift the flour as this removes the bran. Although your baking won't be quite as light and fluffy, you'll find that many of your recipes will taste even better.
- When you buy bread, insist on "100% whole wheat" or the dark rye, and rediscover bread in general—there's fiber in white breads as well.

OTHER HEALTH CONCERNS

Even the best of meals and entertainment can be spoiled by *chewing problems* and food intolerances. If chewing is a problem, don't rely totally on baby foods. Try fish, eggs, cheese, peanut butter, cooked vegetables, stews made with minced meat, soups, some cereals, ice cream, canned fruit. These soft foods, though, are also low in fiber, so they may increase any constipation you may have. The real solution is to see a good dentist to have the problems corrected. If ill-fitting dentures are causing the problem, you don't *have* to live with them!

Heartburn, indigestion and other signs of food intolerances may also increase as we grow older. Some basic changes are taking place in our bodies which allow acid to flow up out of the stomach to cause heartburn. The rate at which food materials move through our bodies slows down, resulting in gas and a feeling of bloatedness. Smaller, more frequent meals and a reasonable amount of fiber will help this.

The amount of enzymes that we produce which digest fat and carbohydrates (particularly milk sugar or lactose) also decreases with age. This means we may have to cut back slightly on the total fat we eat. Try not to cut out milk and milk products, however; they have the calcium you need. Products that break down lactose to other easily absorbed sugars are available, if you find milk difficult to digest. If you can't find them at your pharmacy, check with your doctor or the dietary department of your local hospital.

You may find that no matter how you try, there are some foods you cannot eat. Don't worry. As long as you're not eliminating whole groups of foods such as milk or fruits, you can still plan a good diet for yourself from the abundance of good foods available.

SHORTCUTS TO A HEALTHY DIET

It may be difficult to follow some of the suggestions we have made, for many reasons. Grocery shopping, for instance, may be tiresome and expensive, especially if you're cooking for only one or two. Here are some suggestions to help you establish a sensible, convenient routine:

- To make grocery shopping easier, write up a rough list of what you need for the week. Include foods in season, as they're less expensive.

- If they suit your needs, look for "no name" or house brands.
- To avoid waste, buy smaller cans. They may be more expensive than the large economy sizes—but think about the waste if you can't use all the food.
- If you live alone, shop with a friend and share your food. But don't forget that you can ask the butcher to repackage meat into smaller portions if the available packages contain too much for you. And you can do the same thing for fresh fruits and vegetables.
- Buy only what you can easily carry. You can always go back for more when you feel up to it.
- Reconsider convenience foods. Instant mashed potatoes may be more convenient for you to use from time to time. So can quick rice, pudding mixes, frozen meat entrées and vegetables. Some convenience foods such as TV dinners and prepared stews can be nourishing. They're more expensive but easy to prepare, and they cut down on leftovers.
- Skim milk powder is both economical and nutritious. Reconstitute the powder into fluid milk for drinking, or use it in baking.
- Store foods properly to avoid spoilage. If you have a freezer, freeze bread, rolls, and muffins and take out as needed. Make up your favorite foods—stews, casseroles—and freeze them in meal-size portions.

To liven up your eating—and your day—eat a good breakfast. You've got the time now, and you'll feel "peppier" if you start the day right. It doesn't have to be bacon and eggs. Try French toast with applesauce, or oatmeal with juice and milk, even grilled cheese on toast, fruit nut bread, and cocoa.

Try to steer clear of the "tea and toast" syndrome. If you're retired, you have more time to plan meals and shop at off-peak hours. Cooking classes are springing up in a lot of community centers. Why not consider enrolling in one and learning how to create new recipes?

Invite a friend or neighbor to join you for lunch or dinner. Or start up a "diners' club" that meets for lunch once or twice a month at a new restaurant (lunch menus are far less expensive than dinner).

If the weather's good, take a brisk walk before a meal—it will perk up your appetite. Or walk through an indoor mall—even through the corridors of your apartment building. Then select a pleasant spot to eat, by a window or on a balcony if it's warm enough. Set a pretty table: a colorful place mat, a few flowers, your favorite china make quite a difference. And change the time of day you eat your main meal. (Some people are more tired at the end of a day and skip cooking dinner as a result).

This may all seem like a lot of effort. But as the saying goes—you're worth it.

General Index

217